French in Michigan

DISCOVERING THE PEOPLES OF MICHIGAN

Russell M. Magnaghi, *Series Editor*
Arthur W. Helweg and Linwood H. Cousins, *Founding Editors*

Ethnicity in Michigan: Issues and People
Jack Glazier and Arthur W. Helweg

African Americans in Michigan
Lewis Walker, Benjamin C. Wilson,
Linwood H. Cousins

Albanians in Michigan
Frances Trix

Amish in Michigan
Gertrude Enders Huntington

Arab Americans in Michigan
Rosina J. Hassoun

Asian Indians in Michigan
Arthur W. Helweg

Belgians in Michigan
Bernard A. Cook

Chaldeans in Michigan
Mary C. Sengstock

Copts in Michigan
Eliot Dickinson

Cornish in Michigan
Russell M. Magnaghi

Danes and Icelanders in Michigan
Howard L. Nicholson, Anders J. Gillis,
and Russell M. Magnaghi

Dutch in Michigan
Larry ten Harmsel

Finland-Swedes in Michigan
Mika Roinila

Finns in Michigan
Gary Kaunonen

French in Michigan
Russell M. Magnaghi

French Canadians in Michigan
John P. DuLong

Germans in Michigan
Jeremy W. Kilar

Greeks in Michigan
Stavros K. Frangos

Haitians in Michigan
Michael Largey

Hmong Americans in Michigan
Martha Aladjem Bloomfield

Hungarians in Michigan
Éva V. Huseby-Darvas

Irish in Michigan
Seamus P. Metress and Eileen K. Metress

Italians in Michigan
Russell M. Magnaghi

Jews in Michigan
Judith Levin Cantor

Latinos in Michigan
David A. Badillo

Latvians in Michigan
Silvija D. Meja

Lithuanians in Michigan
Marius K. Grazulis

Maltese in Michigan
Joseph M. Lubig

Mexicans and Mexican Americans in Michigan
Rudolph Valier Alvarado and Sonya Yvette Alvarado

Norwegians in Michigan
Clifford Davidson

Poles in Michigan
Dennis Badaczewski

Scandinavians in Michigan
Jeffrey W. Hancks

Scots in Michigan
Alan T. Forrester

Serbians in Michigan
Paul Lubotina

South Slavs in Michigan
Daniel Cetinich

Swedes in Michigan
Rebecca J. Mead

Yankees in Michigan
Brian C. Wilson

Discovering the Peoples of Michigan is a series of publications examining the state's rich multicultural heritage. The series makes available an interesting, affordable, and varied collection of books that enables students and educated lay readers to explore Michigan's ethnic dynamics. A knowledge of the state's rapidly changing multicultural history has far-reaching implications for human relations, education, public policy, and planning. We believe that Discovering the Peoples of Michigan will enhance understanding of the unique contributions that diverse and often unrecognized communities have made to Michigan's history and culture.

French
in Michigan

Russell M. Magnaghi

Michigan State University Press

East Lansing

♾ The paper used in this publication meets the minimum requirements of
ANSI/NISO Z39.48-1992 (R 1997) (Permanence of Paper).

Michigan State University Press
East Lansing, Michigan 48823-5245

Printed and bound in the United States of America.

25 24 23 22 21 20 19 18 17 16   1 2 3 4 5 6 7 8 9 10

Magnaghi, Russell M.
French in Michigan / Russell M. Magnaghi.
pages cm
Includes bibliographical references and index.
ISBN 978-1-61186-198-3 (pbk. : alk. paper)—ISBN 978-1-60917-484-2 (pdf)—
ISBN 978-1-62895-259-9 (ebook)—ISBN 978-1-62896-259-8 (kindle) 1. French Americans—
Michigan—History. 2. French Americans—Michigan—Social life and customs. 3. French Americans—
Michigan—Social conditions. 4. Immigrants—Michigan—History. 5. French—Michigan—History.
6. Michigan—Ethnic relations. 7. Michigan—Social life and customs. 8. Michigan—Social conditions.
I. Title.
F575.F8M333 2007
305.8009774—dc23
2015017983

Interior and cover design by Charlie Sharp, Sharp Des!gns, Lansing, MI
Cover image of the L'Huillier & Proulx store in Marquette (1899). Courtesy of Robert Bordeau.

Michigan State University Press is a member of the Green Press Initiative and is
committed to developing and encouraging ecologically responsible publishing
practices. For more information about the Green Press Initiative and the use of
recycled paper in book publishing, please visit *www.greenpressinitiative.org*.

Visit Michigan State University Press at *www.msupress.org*

Contents

Preface

The study of the French in the United States has been hampered by a lack of appreciation for how much of American culture and life has been influenced by the French. As historian and author David McCullough has frequently stated in writings and a talk to the John F. Kennedy Foundation in June 2012, Americans do not appreciate the deep relationship between the United States and France. French support during the American Revolution was critical, French names are scattered across a map of the United States, and Napoleon's sale of Louisiana in 1803 doubled the size of the United States. Then there is the gift of the Statue of Liberty from France and our participation in two world wars and the sixty thousand Americans buried in the military cemeteries in France. Despite these strong developments and ties, Americans tend to have a lack of understanding of the role of France in our history and certainly the history of Michigan.

With my own awareness of McCullough's observations, I readily accepted the invitation extended by Arthur Helweg, professor at Western Michigan University and editor of Michigan State University Press's Discovering the Peoples of Michigan series, on a cold February day in 2003 to write about the influence of France and its people on the state of Michigan. It has been a challenge and a form of discovery that demanded extensive research because relatively very little had been written about French immigration in Michigan history in books and journal articles especially focusing on the nineteenth century or it had been "lost" in poorly indexed journals.

The French Canadians in Michigan have been chronicled in this series by John DuLong, and it is not my intention to repeat that fine story.[1] Here I focus on the contributions of immigrants born in France proper, who first came with the French Canadians and developed Michigan. After laying the colonial foundations, I focus on carefully digging into the French-born immigrant story in the nineteenth, twentieth, and early twenty-first centuries. The story is there, but it emerges only after piecing together many minute sources—census data, reports, archival sources, and whatever I could uncover and analyze.

Despite my Italian surname, I can claim half of my ancestry as French. The work is a tribute to Catherine Claverie and Martin Mendiara, my maternal grandparents, who lived their French heritage and language. They were French and French Basque respectively, from the Department Pyrénées-Atlantiques, a region that sent many of its youth to the Americas starting with Pierre Laclede (1729-78), the founder of St. Louis, Missouri, and continuing with immigrants who went to California during the Gold Rush. Although they did not settle in Michigan but in California, their daughter Grace and their grandson were and are residents of this state. This monograph commemorates the arrival of my grandparents—Catherine in 1904 and Martin in 1906—to the United States.

This work has seen the author track down bits of information from numerous archives and libraries in the state. The digging for information was greatly aided by the staffs of the Bentley Historical Library of the University of Michigan; Burton Historical Collection of the Detroit Public Library; the Library of Michigan, Lansing; Archives of the Diocese of Marquette; and the Northern Michigan University Archives. The staffs of the Walter Reuther Library; Sisters of St. Joseph, Carondelet, St. Louis, Missouri; and Robert Bordeau have been helpful in locating and providing photographs for this study. Rebecca Kessler has been extremely helpful editing the original manuscript that produced the following result. Without her assistance this work would remain in a file. My wife, Diane, as usual has kept me on top of the project and seen to its completion. A grand thank you to everyone. Now the story of the French in Michigan, one of the few state histories dealing with this ethnic group, can reach publication.

Introduction

The French Republic (République française) occupies 212,918 square miles and is the largest nation in Western Europe. Outside of the Pyrenees in the south and the Alps in the southeast, the terrain of France varies from mountain ranges to plains to forests and includes four major river systems. As a result of this and its central location, France has proven a prosperous nation over the centuries.

France has had a varied history as well. Home to Celtic people, it was conquered by the Romans under Julius Caesar and was known as Gaul. In the years that followed it was a major component in the Roman Empire and then was invaded by barbarians. Around 700 Charlemagne was the first unifying force to pull the disparate parts together, but this unity did not last beyond his reign. France then fell into small political entities and struggled to keep itself from being absorbed by the English. This large and wealthy nation was divided among rival kingdoms, and problems followed.

So how did France come to play a major role in European history and be at the forefront of intellectual and social developments? It was Louis xiv, the "Sun King," who dominated the scene in the late seventeenth and early eighteenth centuries. Besides putting France on the cultural European map, he played a major role in European military and diplomatic affairs. Louis also developed a grand empire that included colonial Michigan.

How did the French approach the North American heartland and Michigan? Given their weak political organization, the French were unable to develop a colonial empire in the early sixteenth century. At that time French fishermen from the coastal ports sailed for the Grand Banks of Newfoundland where they fished for cod that was salted and became a major component in the French and European diet. These fishermen soon learned that the local Native Americans had furs that could be traded and were more valuable than codfish. The fur trade had begun. After several successful and unsuccessful attempts to settle Atlantic Canada, the French under Samuel de Champlain moved down the St. Lawrence River and founded Quebec City in 1608. It was under the founder of New France that the French moved inland, explored, developed the fur trade, and evangelized the Native Americans beginning in the early seventeenth century. This conquest of North America was expanded during the reign of Louis XIV.

During the eighteenth century France became prosperous and the most populous country in Europe, going from 21.5 million citizens in 1700 to 27.5 million eighty years later. Its closest rivals population-wise were Russia with about twelve million and England with between five and six million. Despite this population and the fact that France was expanding into varied regions of the world, from America to Africa and India, and into Michigan, French immigrants were reluctant to leave France. During the colonial era, hundreds of Frenchmen from the Atlantic provinces of Brittany and Normandy found their way to New France (Canada) primarily due to their proximity to the sea. However the country had a relative homogeneous population, and French Protestants like the Huguenots, who would have willingly left the country, were either suppressed or not allowed to colonize. The country had vast areas of arable farmland whose titles remained in the hands of the peasants who clung tenaciously to the land. Furthermore, the country was early connected by a fine transportation system that allowed goods to easily pass to areas where they were in demand. Adding to this was the development of its base as a major industrial power in Europe. The French army was large due to France's continental location and military concerns. As a result it is plausible that employment opportunities in the army reduced the number of potential immigrants. Besides these physical developments, intellectual life blossomed in the eighteenth century in the hands of *philosophes* (philosophers), with France leading the way in the intellectual life of Europe.

Although France exuded the look of a prosperous, well-developed nation, there were economic and social problems that were highlighted by the *philosophes*, discussed at length, and then led to the French Revolution beginning in 1789. Overall these strong points in France kept the population within the boundaries of the nation from leaving. It was the radical social change that came about during the Revolution that forced émigrés— nobles, craftsmen, and Catholic clergy—to emigrate or lose their heads to the guillotine.

French emigration to New France had been a serious problem as early as the colonial period ending in 1763. The emigrants who arrived were faced with wars against the Iroquois and the New Englanders that kept the colonists on security alert and made daily life tension-filled. As a result of this tension there were instances of as many as 70 percent of French emigrants returning to France soon after their arrival. As a result New France, compared to New England, was sparsely populated. In 1763 when France left North America there were 70,000 French Canadians who remained, between Quebec in the north and Louisiana in the south, while the English colonies had a population of 1.6 million Anglophones.

Despite the strong forces that kept French people at home, some French did immigrate to the United States primarily during the nineteenth century. The typical immigrant left as an individual or as part of a family seeking change or economic opportunity. Understanding the history of French immigration to the United States and specifically Michigan is tricky. We have to deal with faulty immigration figures. At times French immigrants have been inflated by officials counting as "French" all European immigrants whose port of departure for North American shores was France. Figures have also been inflated by the inclusion of French Canadians, Acadians, Caribbean French, and Cajuns as "French." Also, official figures were kept low by French authorities in order to downplay the out-migration of Frenchmen.

Characterizing French immigrants, historian Laurie Collier has concluded:

> Despite these relative small numbers, French immigrants have tended to
> be more successful and influential than other groups in America. French
> immigrants are generally urban, middleclass, skilled, and progressive, and
> they are more likely to be employed as artisans and merchants.[2]

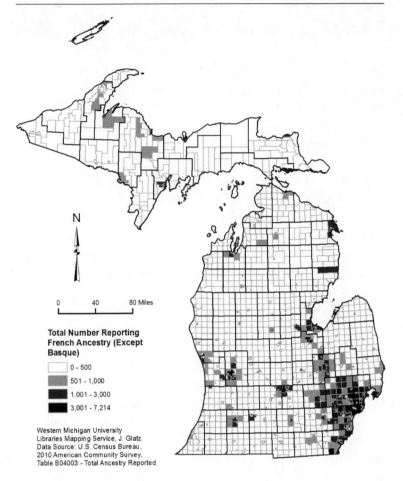

N

0   40   80 Miles

Total Number Reporting French Ancestry (Except Basque)

☐ 0 - 500
▨ 501 - 1,000
▨ 1,001 - 3,000
■ 3,001 - 7,214

Western Michigan University
Libraries Mapping Service, J. Glatz
Data Source: U.S. Census Bureau,
2010 American Community Survey,
Table B04003 - Total Ancestry Reported

This will be an important characteristic to be found among the French immigrants who settled in Michigan beginning in the years after the American occupation of the future state in 1796 and commences the study. The anchor point is the 1850 federal census that provides place of nativity for the first time. Between 1796 and 1850, Michigan had attracted 945 French immigrants, although some of them had arrived prior to 1796. It is important to note the contrast of immigration from the Netherlands (2,542) and from Ireland (13,430) to Michigan by 1850. The first nation was tiny compared to France's landmass and faced religious problems, while Ireland was both

French Immigration to Michigan, 1850–1950

Year	Population	Year	Population	Year	Population
1850	945	1890	5,182	1930	4,581
1860	2,446	1900	2,590	1940	3,364
1870	3,121	1910	2,410	1950	3,632
1880	3,203	1920	4,174		

small and faced the devastating potato famine that drove thousands from the countryside. In both cases the immigrants had a reason to leave.

The census data between 1850 and 1950 are a fine indication of French attitudes toward leaving France.[3] As a result, there were decades of modest increases and then serious decreases as between 1890 and 1900 when the state lost 50 percent of its French immigrants for an unknown reason (see table). During the years between 1910 and 1920 the largest increase of the hundred-year period took place due to the developing automobile industry and a demand for workers, with an increase of 1,764 French immigrants. A review of more detailed census data shows that the French immigrant population was rather evenly located throughout the state, with much higher concentration in Wayne County and Detroit and in the neighboring counties although the population spiked in Houghton and Marquette Counties in the Upper Peninsula at certain periods.

Colonial Era in Michigan

For Michigan the French colonial era lasted from the 1620s through 1763 and had a number of important components. The first of these was the role of explorers who defined the Great Lakes region as one of the newer parts of the French Empire. Names like Etienne Brulé, Pierre-Esprit Radisson, Médard des Groseilliers, Duluth, and a host of Jesuit missionaries are associated with the exploration of this region.

Explorers

The first French explorers into the Great Lakes country were seeking gold and a route to the South Sea or the Pacific and ultimately Asia. In the 1620s Etienne Brulé, having been trained by the Indians, visited the region and noted the potential fur trade. He was followed by Jean Nicolet in 1634 who got as far as Green Bay seeking the route to China. Soon after Pierre-Esprit Radisson and Médard des Groseilliers entered the Lake Superior country and outlined the advantages of the subsequent development of the fur trade and the role of the Hudson Bay connection.

Jesuit missionaries whose main task was to evangelize the Indians also observed the environment and the people and recorded their observations.

From water-level observations, by 1671 two Jesuits, Claude-Jean Allouez and
Claude Dablon, created an accurate map of Lake Superior that was soon
published. A few military men like Antoine Laumet Lamothe, Sieur de Cadillac left their observations as well.[4]

All of this exploration led to the French establishing territorial claim
to the region. The economic minister or intendant, Jean Talon (1626–94),
concerned about ownership of the Great Lakes region, sent Simon François,
Sieur de St. Lusson (died after 1677), a military officer and deputy, to Sault
Ste. Marie. He was ordered to claim Lakes Huron and Superior and all of
the lands adjacent and beyond, both discovered and undiscovered, for Louis
XIV. St. Lusson oversaw an elaborate ceremony, called "The Pageant of the
Sault" at Sault Ste. Marie on June 14, 1671. Indian representatives of dozens
of tribes and villages were invited to and witnessed the ceremony. Troops
in formal uniforms stood at attention while the French royal standard and
a cross were erected on a hillside and the land claimed for the king without
getting Indian approval for his action. Then Jesuit Father Claude Allouez
presented a unique homily to the Indians, showing them in Native terms the
power and might of their new ruler, Louis XIV, into whose empire they had
entered and could not leave without a terrible struggle.

René-Robert Cavelier, Sieur de La Salle (1643–87), was an important
French explorer and entrepreneur in North America. In 1678 he obtained
permission from Louis XIV to explore the Mid-Continent of North America
from the Great Lakes to the Gulf of Mexico, establish forts, develop the fur
trade, make contact with Mexico, and possibly find a route to Asia. He ma-
nipulated this mandate into a colossal scheme to develop an inland empire
with himself as viceroy. A year later, above Niagara Falls, La Salle had the
forty-five-ton sailing vessel *Griffon* constructed, and then he sailed on board
through the Straits of Mackinac into Green Bay. On its return voyage, laden
with twelve thousand pounds of furs, the ship sank somewhere in northern
Lake Michigan. The *Griffon* has numerous stories and legends attached to
it and how and why it sank. Over the years various groups have sought the
wreck of the vessel. The Great Lakes Exploration Group in 2001 felt that they
had found the site. However, legal squabbles among the group, the state
of Michigan, the federal government, and the government of France over
ownership has dragged on with various problems being settled. In a sense
the legend lives on.[5]

Fur Trade

As the land was defined, the fur trader entered the scene as furs were considered the "gold" of the Great Lakes region. This trade brought the region
and its people into the global market, for furs meant riches when demand
was high and poverty when demand was low, constant features both the
French and Indians had to face. The fur trading settlement of Fort Buade
located in the center of modern St. Ignace at the Straits of Mackinac was
the first such post in Michigan. Located at the crossroads of the Great Lakes
it was an entrepôt and headquarters for the French traders and attracted
Indians from great distances. Closed in the 1690s by Louis XIV because of
the glut of furs on the market, it was reestablished in 1715. Located on the
south side of the straits, Fort Michilimackinac continued as the major fur
trading center in the Great Lakes and as a strategic military outpost.[6] In July
1701 Antoine Laumet Lamothe, Sieur de Cadillac founded Fort Pontchartrain
d'troit ("Fort Pontchatrain at the Narrows" of the Detroit River). This settlement along with Michilimackinac became important to the development
of colonial Michigan. A third major trade-military post was Fort St. Joseph
where Niles, Michigan, is today, first founded as a Jesuit mission site in the
1680s. In 1691 the trade-military post was established. In the north, Sault Ste.
Marie, located at an important water entry into the Lake Superior country,
was first founded as St. Mary mission by the Jesuits in 1668 and also became
a fur trading center.

Missionaries

The next important contribution of the French was the introduction of
Christianity to New France in 1632 by Jesuit missionaries belonging to the
Society of Jesus.[7] Beginning in 1641, when French Jesuit priests Isaac Jogues
and Charles Raymbault visited the Ojibwa at Sault Ste. Marie, the Jesuits
worked in the state for over a century. There was a short-lived mission called
Ste. Thérèse at the end of Keweenaw Bay that was founded by Father René
Menard in 1660. The first major mission located at Sault Ste. Marie—St.
Mary's—was founded by Father Jacques Marquette in 1668, the mission
of St. Ignace was founded at the Straits of Mackinac in 1671 followed by a
neighboring mission of St. Francis Borgia, and in the 1680s another mission

was established at the southern end of the state at Niles. At Detroit the first missionaries were Recollet fathers who ministered to both the French and Indians at Detroit. This proved to be a disaster for the Hurons, who drifted away from the faith. In 1728 the Jesuit Armand de la Richardie (1686–1758) was sent to Detroit to establish the mission of Notre-Dame-de-l'Assomption among the Hurons. His patient devotion worked, and by 1735 there were six hundred neophyte Christians. Evangelization was plagued with Indian unrest and intrigue by English traders. The mission was moved twenty miles down the Detroit River to Bois Blanc Island, and eventually it became the first Catholic parish in Ontario across the river.[8]

The Jesuits established Ste. Anne church within the walls of Fort Michilimackinac after 1715 and the closure of St. Ignace mission across the straits. In 1742 they established a mission outpost for the Odawa at Cross Village southwest of Fort Michilimackinac.

The Jesuit missionaries were active throughout the state. In contrast to other mission experiences, the Jesuits in Michigan allowed the Indians to remain in their villages with the missions established nearby. They used the missions as headquarters, visiting and ministering to the Indians in their villages and staying with them during the long, cold winter months. The missionaries provided the Indians with basic religious instruction and education, medical assistance, and agricultural instruction. At times they had to face hostility between various Indian tribes and tried to maintain the peace.

Farmers and Farming

The first European-style farming and crops were introduced by the French missionaries and settlers. The missionaries introduced agriculture to the Ojibwa who never practiced farming and new crops to the Odawa and Hurons who were traditional farmers. The missions were usually the source of this farming activity. However in May 1749 a report tells us that the military engineer Joseph-Gaspard Chaussegros de Léry left Montreal accompanying a group of French settlers with "slips of vines, fruit stones, pips, and seeds of all kinds to take to Detroit."[9] The French introduced pears and other fruit along with wheat, oats, peas, onions, chives, and garlic. Some of the pear trees first introduced by the French in Detroit are still flourishing and

producing fruit. The French also brought with them livestock, which proved
to be successful. Jesuit missionary La Richardie oversaw a number of farms
that were developed for and by the Huron Indians around Detroit in the
1740s and 1750s.

Chroniclers

Not satisfied with introducing farming, crops, and livestock, the missionaries
wrote of the environment and its botanical assets. Father Marquette wrote in
detail about wild rice and how the Indians grew, harvested, and processed
the staple. Others wrote about other native plants like rock tripe, a lichen
that was used during times of famine, blueberries, and acorns. In 1721 Father
Pierre Charlevoix wrote extensively about Michigan's environment and
people. Much of this information can be found in the *Jesuit Relations* that
were seventeenth- and eighteenth-century reports about the work of the
Jesuits that were sent to France and published.[10]

Laymen also left accounts of the Michigan environment. Cadillac was
commandant at Fort Michilimackinac when he wrote beginning in the 1690s
about his experiences at the Straits of Mackinac and later at Detroit.[11] Other
commandants also wrote of their experiences and the land and its resources.
One of the more detailed accounts comes from the pen of Louis-Armand
de Lom d'Arce de Lahonton (1666–1716), who wrote extensively about his
experiences in the Great Lakes region. Although there were no French
scientists in Michigan during the colonial era, Jacques-Pierre Daneau de
Muy (1695–1758), born in Canada with strong European ties, played a role as
military leader and botanist. In the fall of 1730 he was given command of Fort
St. Joseph at what is now Niles, Michigan. His official duties were to maintain
trade and keep the neighboring Potawatomi and Miami as allies. Although
we do not know his training, his strong interest in botany allowed him to
make a close study of plants in the area, primarily seeking pharmaceutical
knowledge. He sent back plant specimens to the intendant at Quebec City
for his inspection and for the Jesuits to classify. His knowledge and skill with
local herbs apparently allowed him to cure several Indians. De Muy left the
post after five years, and when he was sent to France he took with him a
memorandum of his findings and a large collection of specimens to be ana-
lyzed by scientists for their medicinal properties.[12]

Settlements

So far we have seen the development of missions, fur trading, and military posts, but it should be remembered that these communities also attracted settlers. The majority of the French colonial settlers to Michigan were born in New France, but a small number came directly from France through Quebec. Detroit, the largest community between Montreal and New Orleans, had a growing population of eight hundred in 1765. Most of the habitants were soldiers, merchants, fur trader, or farmers or a mixture of the group. Many of the French settlers in the Detroit area settled along the northeast coast of Detroit—modern Grosse Pointe. Here they developed narrow ribbon farms along Lake St. Clair and the Detroit River, which eased transportation concerns by using canoes in the summer and sleds on the iced river in the winter.

Many of the early settlers came as adventurers or as army officers and soldiers and decided to remain in their new homes. This was true of Louis Beaufait who married and developed a farm in Grosse Pointe. Jean Chapaton, army surgeon, retired and developed a farm in Detroit. A notable Frenchman was Robert Navarre (1709–91) who was born in France and educated in Paris, and when he arrived in Detroit became the French notary public, in charge of witnessing the signing of legal documents. In 1736 he was responsible for collecting taxes and later for dealing with personal and property matters, much as a probate judge does today. He was familiar with local Indian languages and often served as an official interpreter. He held this position and that of post storekeeper until 1759. With the coming of British rule in 1760 after the loss of the French and Indian War, Navarre continued as notary. He may have been the author of the manuscript *Journal of Pontiac's Conspiracy, 1763*, an account of Odawa leader Pontiac's uprising in 1763 that served as the historical basis of Francis Parkman's early work, *The Conspiracy of Pontiac*.[13] Navarre spent his later years with his wife, Marie Lothman de Barrois, on land granted him by the French government in 1747. He passed away in Detroit in 1791 after an extremely active and noteworthy career, and today his descendants are located throughout southeast Michigan.

If it was difficult to attract men to New France, fewer women arrived. The first intendant or economic minister, Jean Talon, was instructed to develop all aspects of the colony. After his arrival in 1666 he organized the colonial economy and offered inducements for early marriage and large families. Groups of usually orphan girls known as *les filles du roi* were sent from France and quickly found husbands in New France. The population that stood at 3,215 at that time rose to 6,000 within a few years. It was difficult to get French women born in Canada and those born in France to venture into the western frontier and the settlements of Michigan. For lack of "appropriate" white brides the men took Native brides. Some Frenchmen with social connections were able to marry French Canadian women in Montreal or Quebec. At one point Cadillac unsuccessfully lobbied for "Christianized" Indian women from Michilimackinac to be brought to Detroit as brides, but the Jesuits opposed his plan. The Indian, métis (mixed Indian and French ancestry), or French women on the Michigan frontier brought with them a civilizing influence. They also cleared and cultivated the fields and planted vegetable gardens and orchards, especially if their husbands were away fur trading. These young women processed and preserved foodstuffs and became successful farm managers. Some of them became involved in the fur trade and other business interests. The women raised families of as many as a dozen children and, lacking schools, taught them at home and passed on folk traditions and religion. They also became "doctors," using Native remedies along with a store of European medicines and lore when they or their children were ill. At times women protected their households against Indian attacks.

The life of Marie-Thérèse Guyon Cadillac is an example of a French woman on the Michigan frontier. After her husband founded Detroit in 1701 she decided to join him despite the difficulties of canoe travel on the Great Lakes. She left two daughters in a convent at Quebec. She and Marie-Anne de Tonty, traveling with Madame Cadillac's seven-year-old son, were the first European women to travel west. They arrived in Detroit in May 1702. Native Americans were surprised to see these first French women. The women quickly transformed Detroit into a proper settlement. Madame Cadillac took control of her husband's business affairs, especially when he had to travel to Montreal, and she served as doctor to the two hundred habitants and four thousand Native Americans living in the vicinity. The Cadillacs had six or seven children while at Detroit before Marie left in 1710.[14]

The French and Indian War, as it is called in the Americas, is known by Europeans as the Seven Years' War. The war pitted the French and their

Native allies against the English on many fronts. Unfortunately the French were defeated outside the walls of Quebec City on the Plains of Abraham in September 1760. It took a while, but in 1763 according to the Treaty of Paris the French claim to North America was relinquished to the English. In Michigan the French and French Canadians remained, if they desired, as did the métis. As a result of this turn of events New France, known to Voltaire as "the ice box," which never attracted many French immigrants, was no longer a destination for French immigrants during the English era that ended in 1796.

What did the French in Michigan think of the American Revolution and associated events? They heard of and some were involved in the western events of the American Revolution such as a George Rogers Clark invasion with his Kentucky force. They saw Fort Mackinac built on Mackinac Island and fortifications improved at Detroit. A feared American invasion never took place although some western tribes were partial to the Americans. Then another Treaty of Paris (1783), which ended the American Revolution, gave the newly formed United States all of the land in the Great Lakes country, but the English refused to give up this economic center of the fur trade and remained. Life for the French did not change during these years. Finally, after a series of Indian wars and Jay's Treaty, the English left the region in 1796, and suddenly the American phase began the onset of the nineteenth century.

Nineteenth-Century French Immigration

The early years of the century saw a number of French—laymen and clergy—play significant roles in the development of Michigan. Detroit was the major settlement on the western frontier at the advent of the nineteenth century.[15] As a result it was the destination of some French émigrés fleeing the violence of the French Revolution, which began in 1789. At the same time Joel Barlow, representing American interests, officially organized the Compagnie du Scioto. False advertising promoted the sale of worthless deeds to lands in eastern Ohio to prospective settlers, companies, and individuals in France, many of whom were aristocrats and associated craftsmen who wanted to leave France. In May 1791, 218 French folks arrived at Alexandria, Virginia, only to learn of the fraud. Some returned to France, others settled in eastern cities, but fifty traveled to lands in Ohio. During the 1790s, many of the French settlers, having exhausted their funds, left the town of Gallipolis and moved to more populous settlements. Detroit, with its French origins and located some 250 miles to the north on the Sandusky-Scioto Trail, was the destination for some of these unfortunate people.

Fortunately the biographical study of one of these settlers exists. One of the earliest French immigrants to settle in Detroit after the American occupation in 1796 was Pierre-Jean Desnoyers (1772–1846), a skilled craftsman.[16] Born in Paris, he worked as a silversmith for his father until he was eighteen

years old. The French Revolution was raging, and his father thought it best
that he leave France and go to America where he would have better opportunity; to help his son he bought him a deed to land owned by the Scioto Land
Company. Desnoyers sailed for America and arrived in May 1791 and soon
learned that his father had been swindled and the deed was worthless. He
moved to Pittsburgh where he could ply his trade, and in the late 1790s he
relocated to Detroit. The United States government contracted with him, and
he worked as an armorer until 1803. After that he went into business for himself and did a brisk business making medals for the Indian trade and other
items that were in demand. He continued in business operating a general
store and silversmithing works; in 1822 as demand for medals declined he
devoted himself to the mercantile trade until his retirement in 1835. As the
settlement expanded he bought lands in 1819 and 1821 in what would become
Bloomfield Hills and Southfield.

Desnoyers was a lay equivalent of Father Gabriel Richard in terms of his
commitment to the community. During the War of 1812 he played a number
of important roles rescuing prisoners and seeing that the Americans had
gunpowder. Later he served as a Wayne County commissioner, alderman
at large for the city of Detroit, and ward alderman, and he along with Father
Richard was one of the first trustees on the Board of Regents of the University
of Michigan. Finally in 1818 he bought shares in the Bank of Michigan and
went on to serve as a director and then president of the bank. His son Peter Jr.
followed in his father's footsteps and had a successful business and political
career in Detroit and was state treasurer (1839–40).[17]

A second prominent French-born citizen of early American Detroit was
Peter Audrain (1725–1820),[18] who left France to join Baron von Steuben and
fight in the American Revolution in 1777. He served with Baron von Steuben
for two years, until poor health brought about his retirement to Philadelphia.
In June 1796 he joined General Anthony Wayne and his men when they first
occupied Detroit. Audrain kept a short journal of this trip westward.[19] He
began his governmental career when General Wayne named him notary
for Wayne County, which covered the entire the state of Michigan and as
far west as the Mississippi River. He served as probate judge in Detroit
(1796–1809) and was also city registrar, clerk of courts, secretary to the land
board, and secretary to the territorial judges. During the War of 1812, he was
pro-American, had his house in Detroit plundered by the British, and was

forced to a farm south of town. He was known for his fine penmanship and
continued in his duties until old age forced him to retire in 1819.

Clergy

If the French Revolution threatened aristocrats and their associated craftsmen with deportation or execution, the Catholic clergy were not exempt.
The Catholic Church had been closely identified with the monarchy and
thus came under attack. Church lands were nationalized, monasteries suppressed, and after 1790 the clergy were required to take an oath of loyalty to
the constitution or lose their position and pay. Later clergy and laymen who
remained loyal to the church were seen as traitors and counterrevolution-
aries. Some were executed for their faith, and over one hundred priests fled
to the United States.

A small group of priests of the Order of St. Sulpice, whose ministry was
to train priests, was sent to Baltimore, Maryland, to develop St. Mary's
Seminary. A number of these French priests were sent by Bishop John
Carroll to the Midwest—Kentucky, Illinois, Michigan—to minister to the
French-speaking Catholic population. After the American occupation of
the Great Lakes region in 1796, a couple of these priests—Michael Levadoux
(1746–1815) and Gabriel Richard (1767–1832)—were reassigned to Michigan,
and in 1798 they were joined by Jean Dilhet (1753–1811). Father Levadoux
arrived in Detroit in 1796, as parish priest of Ste. Anne's church, soon after
the U.S. Army secured control of the territory. He admired the United States
and promoted the new American spirit among the French. His singing a Te
Deum commemorating the death of President Washington delighted the
local Protestants. Before he was resigned and returned to France, Father
Levadoux ministered to Catholics from Sandusky, Ohio, to Mackinac Island.

Father Jean Dilhet joined the Detroit ministry in 1798 and was assigned
to the parish at River Raisin (modern Monroe). His temperament was unfit
for the rugged American frontier and he antagonized his parishioners, so
he left in 1804 for Detroit. During his last nine years in the United States,
before being reassigned to France, Father Dilhet wrote a manuscript, "État
de l'eglise catholique ou diocèse des États-Unis de l'Amérique septentrionale" (State of the Catholic Church or the Diocese of the U.S.A.). It was not
translated and published until 1922.[20]

Gabriel Richard, Catholic priest and émigré, fled revolutionary France and settled in Detroit, where he became a well-respected community leader and one of the founders of the University of Michigan in 1817. He was also one of two Catholic priests to ever serve in the U.S. Congress.

A third outstanding French immigrant was Father Gabriel Richard. As the distinguished Michigan historian Willis F. Dunbar stated in 1965, "[Gabriel] Richard would become one of the most important forces for cultural and educational advancement in the early history of Michigan."[21] Richard's first concern was for his congregation, which included French, Irish, and German members in Michigan and Wisconsin, and at one point he even ministered to the Protestants in Detroit at their invitation. When Detroit was destroyed by fire in June 1805, although Father Richard lost his home and Ste. Anne's church, he found time to help and comfort the homeless. He also wrote the city motto, still in use: *Speramus meliora resurget cinebus* or "We hope for better things, it will arise from ashes."

One of his chief concerns was the education of the youth of Michigan. As early as 1806 he petitioned the territorial governor and judges for a parcel of land for a proposed "college." He established a vocational training school for Native Americans south at Springwells. In 1817 he and the Presbyterian minister Reverend John Monteith established the embryonic University of Michigan in Detroit. He served as vice president (1817–21) and was a member of the board of trustees until his death.

Father Richard brought the first printing press to Michigan, and the first book off the press was a child's spelling book. In 1809 he published periodicals in French, *Essais du Michigan,* and in English as *The Michigan Essay, or Impartial Observer.*

During the War of 1812 Father Richard remained with his congregation in Detroit and worked to protect the lives and property of American citizens against British reprisals and Indian attacks. When he refused to violate his oath to the U.S. Constitution, the British imprisoned him. However the anti-American Indian leader Tecumseh refused to fight with the British until Richard was released.

In November 1823, with the solid support of the French population, Richard was elected a territorial delegate to the U.S. House of Representatives (1823–25). Although he rarely spoke in Congress, he promoted a number of beneficial projects for the territory, including the Chicago Road linking Detroit and Chicago, which exists today as US-12. His French accent and odd clerical dress made him a curiosity in Washington, and both President James Madison and Secretary of War John C. Calhoun were fascinated by his stories of the Indians of Michigan. Father Richard was the only Catholic priest to serve in Congress until the election of Father Robert Drinan from Massachusetts in 1970. Since the Catholic Church no longer allows priests to run for public office, Father Richard will be one of two to serve in that capacity in the U.S. Congress.

In July 1832 Asiatic cholera arrived in Detroit and spread through the territory. In September Father Richard, ever community-focused, succumbed to either the disease or exhaustion caused by nursing and comforting the sick and dying. So ended the life of one of Michigan's true pioneers and founding fathers.[22]

Besides these French priests, there were others who ministered to the Native Americans and French in southwestern Michigan. They worked among the Potawatomi Indians at the site of a former Jesuit mission on the banks of the St. Joseph River in modern Niles. One of them was Father Stephen T. Badin (1768–1853),[23] a Sulpician seminarian who fled the Revolution. After completing his studies he was the first Catholic priest ordained in the United States. He proceeded to minister to the scattered Catholic population in Kentucky and the Ohio Valley before moving to southwestern Michigan to work with the Potawatomi (1830–33). Father Badin has been given credit with helping to prevent the Catholic Pokagon Band of the Potawatomi, as the

Niles community is now known, from being removed to Kansas as the rest of
the tribe was under the Treaty of Chicago (1833).

A Belgian priest ministered to the Potawatomi tribe after Father Badin
left and was followed by another French priest, Father Benjamin Petit, who
quickly learned their language and culture and was seen by the Indians as a
person who cared about them. In the fall of 1838 he accompanied the tribe
to Kansas where, like many of the Indians, he succumbed to exhaustion and
illness. He died among the Jesuits in St. Louis, Missouri, at the age of twenty-
seven.

The Association for the Propagation of the Faith was established by Pau-
line Jaricot on May 3, 1822, in Lyon, France, to support world missions with
prayers and financial contributions. Between 1822 and 1832 the Catholic
Church in the United States received 42 percent of its funding from this organization. In Michigan, the Catholic Church also received funding through
a unique system from the sale of bottles of wine and champagne shipped
to the American Fur Company in New York City. For instance, in July 1837
the American Fur Company received thirty-five "baskets" of champagne
identified as belonging to "Father Frederick Baraga," a missionary working in northern Michigan. Letters written in 1843 and 1845 provide some
specific information about these shipments. The firm of De Massiac & Du
Loisson of Piery, France, regularly shipped to Ramsay Crooks, agent of the
company, and included cases of bottles earmarked for Baraga's work. In
November 1843, the firm shipped three hundred bottles of their fine quality
wine, which was sold and put into Baraga's account. This was a rather a
unique method for donating to Baraga's ministry in Michigan as Baraga
was a teetotaler.

In the mid-1840s copper was discovered in Ontonagon and Houghton
counties, and soon immigrant laborers were headed for the mines; many
of them were Catholic French Canadians, Germans, and Irish. As a result
in 1857 the Catholic Diocese of Marquette was established, and there was
a demand for priests for this growing population. French Jesuits returned
to the region where they had worked in the past. One of them, Father Jean-
Baptiste Menet, brought Catholicism to the central Upper Peninsula by
ministering to the Catholics in Marquette and Negaunee in the early 1850s.
Throughout the nineteenth century French priests worked in parishes
throughout the state.

Frenchman John Casabonne first settled in Wyoming before developing a successful sheep ranch in Kenton, Michigan. He was typical of many French immigrants who came to Michigan to farm. (Source: Duncan Township, Michigan)

French Settlers

The first large number of French immigrants entered Michigan during the nineteenth century. They arrived in Michigan as individuals or families seeking economic opportunity but did not come as a mass movement. They settled throughout the state, with the largest concentration in Wayne County and Detroit while neighboring counties like Monroe, Washtenaw, Macomb, Oakland, and St. Clair attracted other large groups.[24] However, there were some French immigrants living on North Manitou and Beaver Islands in Lake Michigan. The copper- and iron-mining regions of the Upper Peninsula attracted French immigrants because of the booming economy.

The occupations held by French immigrants were as varied as the people themselves, with the majority being farmers or farm laborers through the century. In 1860 the French settled around Detroit were primarily engaged in farming. In Washtenaw County with thirty-nine French immigrants, seventeen were farmers or farm laborers, while in St. Clair County two French agricultural communities developed at Swan Creek on Lake St. Clair and at Casco a few miles to the north. The Swan Creek settlement consisted of over two dozen farmers, a grocer, and a blacksmith while the Casco settlement consisted of thirty-six immigrants whose main occupation was farming. French occupations blended into the local economy. Centers of mining saw them engaged in mineral extraction, while other occupations ranged from day laborers to merchants, mechanics, or managerial positions. In a few instances some immigrants found employment as basket weavers and popcorn peddlers. Later they would cluster around the service industry, working in hotels and restaurants. In the larger cities like Detroit, Grand Rapids, and Kalamazoo the variety of jobs was diverse.

French Copper Mining Interests

News of the discovery of copper deposits on the Keweenaw Peninsula in 1844 greatly interested French businessmen. A group of entrepreneurs hired Louis-Édouard Rivot (1820–69), a distinguished professor and mining engineer at École des Mines de Paris, who was known for his work in metallurgy not only from the scientific and didactic perspectives but also from a practical one. In early October 1854 he led a French party to the Keweenaw Peninsula along the shores of Lake Superior. Upon his return to Paris, Rivot presented a report to Cail, Cheylus & Bechenec, local investors.[25] This report was concerned specifically with copper mining concessions on the Keweenaw Peninsula at Agate Harbor, Northern Western, Cliff, and South Cliff and to the south in Ontonagon County at Minesota Mine. The following year, Rivot published his book, *Voyage au Lac Supérieur*.[26] This work primarily covers the geology of the region, but he devoted several pages to describing some of the Keweenaw Peninsula towns and ports that he visited. In 1857 he published another study on the same topic titled *Notice sur le Lac Supérieur, États-Unis d'Amérique*.[27]

These substantial geological reports were read by many French capitalists. However, before French money entered the scene, a number of immigrants settled in Ontonagon County and were employed in the mines while some of the women operated boarding houses.

Then in 1861 a new era began to unfold when the Lafayette Mining Company was incorporated in Paris, and within three years the new company improved the property of the previous owner. They operated the mine until copper prices dropped after the Civil War, when they sold it to the Copper Crown Mining Company.[28]

The most active and elaborate French copper mine was located to the south of Copper Harbor. The Clark Mining Company was established early in 1853 and developed a mine there through the next year. Then on March 20, 1855, Le Societé Françoise des Mines des Cuivres Natif du Lac Supérieur, based in France, purchased the Clark Mine property. The agent for the company was Georges Alonzo Simon Maurice, and Jules Borie was named superintendent. Exploration continued, but there is no record of production.

The French Copper Mining Company was formed, and it purchased the Clark Mine along with the Bell Mining Company, the Agate Harbor Mine, and the Montreal Mine, maintaining them as separate properties.

At this point Ferdinand Bartholomy was named superintendent of the Clark Mine and several improvements were made. In 1859 the mine produced 5.6 tons of copper; in 1860 the output rose to 7.2 tons. The mine location at Manganese Lake south of Copper Harbor consisted of many cabins and even a fountain and gardens. In 1860 Copper Harbor included a small French community consisting of Bartholomy, the superintendent; Marcel Demare, a merchant; and Antoine Fligmore, a clerk. Antoine Flenyea was another clerk, living there with his family, and there were four French miners, one of whom was married.

The Clark Mine and its tiny community carried on even as the property changed owners. On April 10, 1861, Felix H. E. Theroulde deeded the property to Edward A. J. Estivant who continued to operate the mine and shipped copper to his copper rolling works in France. After a long history the Estivant family sold their interest in the mine to the Calumet and Hecla Consolidated Copper Company, thus ending nearly a century of French ownership of copper mines on the Keweenaw Peninsula.[29]

Well before the end of this era, however, a French company involved in Michigan's Copper Country made a noteworthy—and disastrous—impression on global copper markets. After the Panic of 1873, which was an economic depression in the United States and Europe, the price of copper dropped from thirty-five cents per pound to under eleven cents in 1886. The opening and development of mines at Butte, Montana, contributed to the downturn. Hyacinthe Secrétan, secretary of Le Société des Métaux of Paris thought he could solve the problem. The society began in the 1860s as a small manufacturing firm making copper novelties. During the 1870 Franco-Prussian War it prospered manufacturing brass cartridges and by 1887 was one of the largest buyers of copper in Europe, if not the world.

In February 1887 the Société des Métaux joined with large French banks—Crédit Lyonnais, Comptoir National d'Escompte de Paris, and the Rothchilds—to form an organization known as Secrétan Syndicate for its promoter and secretary. The Secrétan Syndicate subscribed a fund between $13 million and $19 million with the intent of cornering the copper market. The organization made contracts with the leading copper companies of the world, including Michigan's Calumet and Hecla Mining Company. Naturally the syndicate's supposedly "simple" plan to corner the world market of copper backfired. The Secrétan Syndicate failed and the Bank of France had to rescue Comptoir National d'Escompte de Paris. The world price of copper was saved by the gradual introduction of copper into the market. The Secrétan Syndicate suffered the fate of all "corners," which are doomed to defeat by the laws of supply and demand.[30]

French Women

In Michigan most of the women were married housewives with various time-consuming tasks to keep them busy. Unmarried women as young as teenagers worked as domestic servants, since many people, especially the wealthy, wanted a "French maid" as a status symbol. A few were music and language teachers while others worked as laundresses, seamstresses, and milliners.

A look at the 1860 census provides some personal views of female occupations at the time. Sixty-three-year-old Mary Goutte was a hotel keeper in Plymouth, and Mary Webber, a fifty-four-year-old widow, was a successful farmer in Redford Township. She was raising a teenaged son and took in a French couple as boarders. There were other French women farming in the township as well. On the shores of Lake St. Clair at Grosse Pointe, widow Mary Ann Zuger was a housewife with three unmarried adult children living with her. The family had apparently done quite well, as Mary Ann owned $5,350 in real estate and had personal finances amounting to $600, all of which was a small fortune for the time. In Detroit Valentine Lafferty, a widow with three small children, was a very successful cattle dealer.

Women Helping Women

In the city of Detroit in 1884 the religious order of Our Lady of Charity of the Good Shepherd of Auger operated the House of the Good Shepherd on West Fort Street. Its specific mission according to the vow taken by the sisters was to work with fallen women and keep them from future temptation. The sisters oversaw these women who were taught to do sewing, lace-making, fine "French" laundering, and cooking as sources of income.

In the mid-nineteenth century various Catholic female religious orders that were founded in France began to enter Michigan at the invitation of bishops who needed the nuns' community-related services. The principal orders were the Daughters of Charity of St. Vincent de Paul (founded in 1633 at Châtillon-les-Dombes), Sisters of the Good Shepherd (founded in 1641 at Caen), Sisters of St. Joseph (founded in 1650 at Le Puy-en-Velay), Sisters of St. Paul of Chartres (founded in 1694 at Levesville-la-Chenard), Society or Madams of the Sacred Heart (founded in 1800 in Paris), Sisters of Notre Dame de Namur (founded in 1803 at Amiens), and Little Sisters of the Poor (founded in 1839 at Servan, Brittany). These came to Michigan to provide much-needed social services, first for the poor and weak and then for others in the form of schools, hospitals, orphanages, homes for delinquent girls and women, and the elderly. They have worked with Catholics and non-Catholics, Native Americans, and African Americans.

The first arrivals in 1850 were the Madams of the Sacred Heart, who opened a girls' school in Detroit that is still in operation. The most recent group of French-founded nuns are the Sisters of St. Paul of Chartres, who established a motherhouse in Marquette in 1963, the first of its kind in the United States. Today the nuns minister in the area and operate the Bishop Noa Home in Escanaba.

One important spin-off is Ascension Health, the largest Catholic and nonprofit health-care provider in the United States. The company was established in Michigan in 1999 by the Daughters of Charity and the Sisters of St. Joseph. A number of the other French-founded congregations continue to provide social services in the state, though they now include women of many nationalities.

French Businesses

French immigrants made their marks on a variety of businesses in Michigan. Chief among them was the French laundry—an important hallmark of French immigrant society nationwide and certainly in San Francisco; Detroit was no exception. The meaning of the term "French laundry" is special but eludes definition in most dictionaries. Over the years it has come to mean not only the laundering, cleaning, dyeing, and repairing of clothing, upholstery, and other household goods, but that the work is done with expertise and an attention to detail.

By 1875 Louis C. Brossy was operating the French Steam Dyeing and Cleaning Works at 62 Randolph Street in Detroit. He advertised that he could clean everything from ostrich plumes to lace curtains and dresses. Around the corner at 273 Jefferson, T. R. Bertrand was the proprietor of the Parisien Steam Laundry. He collected and delivered laces, curtains, fine goods, and specialties "done up in French Style."[31]

Although the early French laundries were operated by Frenchmen, later non-French entrepreneurs in Detroit and elsewhere used the terms "Paris," "Parisian," and "French" to advertise their laundries, cleaners, or dye works as authentic and first-class. For example in 1913 John D. Finley and Charles Rider were proprietors of the Paris Laundry while Martin Kelly operated the Parisian Laundry Company. Not to be ignored, Olga J. Hofvander operated the Parisian Dress Shop, which specialized in exclusive gowns made to order. This use of terms like "French" or "Parisian" continued throughout the twentieth century following the standard set by Louis XIV's quest for style and fashion.

French laundries were hardly the only businesses operated by French immigrants to Michigan. Their success and prominence in the business realm provides a window into their role in the cultural and economic fabric of their new homes. Jacques Goffinet was born in 1824 in Belfort, Alsace, France, and came to the United States in 1851 only to reemigrate to France and finally return in 1865. Upon his return, he found his calling and developed a substantial liquor trade in the vicinity of Larned and Randolph Streets in Detroit. By 1870 he was a wholesaler of wines and liquors and soon after opened the Hotel Goffinet in downtown Detroit.

The L'Huillier & Proulx store in Marquette (1899), which sold groceries, boots, and shoes among other items. Many Frenchmen in Michigan entered the service industry and catered to the community. (Source: Robert Bordeau)

Goffinet became prominent within Detroit's French community, where had many friends. He served two terms as president of the Lafayette Benevolent Society. The First Franco-American Building and Savings Society was founded in October 1869, and within a few months Goffinet was involved with the enterprise. In February 1875 the Hotel Goffinet, decorated with French and American flags, served as the headquarters for the reunion of several hundred French citizens celebrating Mardi Gras. There were even plans to have a New Orleans–styled street "procession" the following year, which never developed. With Goffinet's death in July 1877 a major community force left the scene.[32]

Then there were the Petrequin brothers, Louis and Paul, who were born in France and came to the United States with their parents as boys. They were raised on a farm in rural Michigan, moved to Oakland, California, and in 1877 resettled in Detroit. Here the brothers worked as contractors and builders until the death of Paul in 1882 propelled Louis into real estate. By 1892 he was involved in house sales and rentals and the development of subdivisions.

Immigrant Biographies

In the nineteenth and early twentieth centuries there were a series of French immigrants who left their special marks on the development of Michigan in the areas of mining, photography, education, and farming, and their stories follow. One of these early expatriates, as we have seen, was Louis-Édouard Rivot whose observations had a favorable impact on the development of French mining interests in the state.

In the field of higher education, Louis Fasquelle (1808–62) became an important and well-published language professor at the University of Michigan. Born in France, he was educated at the University of Paris and in Germany. As a teacher of French he immigrated to England, married there, and in 1832 traveled to the United States. In Michigan he bought a farm near Ann Arbor and divided his time between agriculture and giving private French lessons. In 1846 he was appointed to the chair of Modern Languages and Literatures at the University of Michigan. He became the university's first professor of modern languages and offered its first French language instruction. He went on to teach Spanish, Italian, and German. Both he and the university became well known for his 1851 book, *A New Method of Learning the French Language*.[33] Fasquelle went on to write and publish a number of works related to the study of the French language that became very successful and went through many editions.[34]

François A. Artault (1813–75) played a dual role of introducing photography to northern Michigan and promoting mining lands to French investors. A student of the early pioneer of photography, Charles Daguerre, Artault left France for New York City in the early 1840s, opened an outlet for chemical and equipment to produce daguerreotypes, and made his own daguerreotypes. He remained in business until 1852 when he moved to Sault Ste. Marie and opened a general store on Water Street selling dry goods, clothing, imported wines, brandies, and champagnes. While there he met and married Mary Tory. Soon after they moved to Ontonagon, a booming mining society with French residents. He introduced the first daguerreotypes to the Copper Country. In Ontonagon his focus shifted to promoting the copper resources in Paris where he was sent by the Ontonagon Mining Association in the late 1850s. By 1861 he was appointed as an unpaid emigration agent by the Michigan legislature "for the purpose of encouraging, by this means emigration

*Sister St. Protais
Deboille was one of
the foundresses of the
Sisters of St. Joseph
in the United States.
Late in her career she
came to Michigan
and worked for many
years with the Native
Americans at the Holy
Name of Jesus mission
school in Baraga,
Michigan.(Source:
Sisters of St. Joseph of
Carondelet, St. Louis
Province Archives)*

and capital from France and other points in Europe to the Upper Peninsula, as well as other parts of Michigan."[35] As part of this effort he wrote the two short works *Mines du cuivre du comté d'Ontonagon: Lac Supérieur, état du Michigan, États-Unis d'Amérique*, which was published in Paris in 1861, and *Exposé d'un projet de création d'un établissement métallurgique au village d'Ontonagon, sur les bords du lac Supérieur, dans l'État du Michigan* the following year.[36] Upon his return from France he continued his work out of New York City and in 1872 was listed as a "stock or mining broker." He died in Paris in 1876 having lived a unique life as a French immigrant to Michigan.[37]

The life of Sister St. Protais Deboille (1814–92) is an example of the work of one of the French-born nuns who came to Michigan. In January 1836 six sisters left France and sailed to New Orleans, en route to St. Louis. In the latter community, where they established their mother house in the suburb of Carondolet, they began their teaching mission as the first congregation of the Sisters of St. Joseph in the United States.

Among these foundresses was a twenty-two-year-old sister named Sister St. Protais. From 1836 to 1872 Sister St. Protais served as teacher and directress in various schools and orphanages in several states, including Illinois, Pennsylvania, West Virginia, Minnesota, and Missouri. In 1872, after a successful career, she fulfilled her long-standing dream to work with Native Americans. She joined a small group of sisters at the Holy Name of Jesus Mission at Assinins in Baraga County, to minister to the spiritual and corporal needs of the Native community.

For the last twenty years of her life she worked as an instructor and visited the sick and infirm. She had a special skill in preparing simple remedies for the sick. Sister St. Protais was respected by the Indians who attributed extraordinary healing powers to her and placed great confidence in her ability to cure their ailments. She passed away in 1892 after taking a bad fall. She was so beloved by the Native community that they demanded that she be buried in their cemetery.[38]

The life story of Pierre Mettetal (1808–1904) sums up the experience of a French farmer and politician living through the century and how his family continued the French tradition in education. He arrived in Michigan prior to statehood in 1837. He and his older brother, Frederic, were French Huguenots who were born and raised in Étupes, France. Frederic came to the United States in 1822 and settled in Philadelphia. Four years later Pierre joined him. In 1829 Pierre moved to Washington, D.C., where he became a steward in the Spanish embassy, and three years later he was working as a teamster and coachman.

Pierre was a staunch Democrat and while in Washington became a friend of President Andrew Jackson and an acquaintance of Lewis Cass, the former territorial governor of Michigan now secretary of war (1831–36). While in the capital, Pierre saved his earnings with the hope of eventually purchasing a farm.

In the late 1830s Frederic moved to Michigan and bought a farm near Mt. Clemens, and Pierre immediately decided to join his brother. He took his savings and paid $320 for eighty acres of good farmland off Schoolcraft Road half a mile from Grand River Road in Redford Township. This was a wilderness that had to be opened and developed. Pierre blazed a trail to his property and quickly made what he termed a "dugout" of logs built up with sod. He cleared the land, planted a garden, raised his own food, and grew corn to feed his cow.

When he became established as a farmer he constructed a two-story log house. In 1841 he married a French Canadian named Angelique Martine (1816–1911) at Assumption Church in her hometown of Petit Côte, Ontario, across from Detroit. Afterward they crossed the river into Michigan and moved onto the farm.

With his growing family, which eventually included eight children, Pierre continued to clear land and expand his farm. He planted a large orchard of apple, pear, and cherry trees and had a patch of Concord, sweet, and white grapes. The garden was carefully planned with each vegetable and herb in its own plot with paths in between.

Growing wild were a variety of berries that the family gathered and processed. Elderberries, for wine and pies, grew along a creek that crossed the property. In the woods there were large blackberries, gooseberries, and thimbleberries, and along the railroad track wild strawberries flourished.

Angelique was a typical frontier woman who had to care for her large and growing family. She planted a beautiful flower garden, and at the time of her wedding she brought pear seeds, which probably came from trees planted by the earliest French inhabitants of the Detroit River area. Angelique pickled what she called sugar pears whole. She carded and spun wool, knitted socks, gloves, and mittens, wove wool blankets, raised chickens, made rag rugs and carpets, sewed the family's clothing, and dipped candles. In 1850 Pierre built a frame house of seven rooms where they raised their four daughters and four sons.

Pierre was a public-spirited individual. He served a term as a juror, walking eight miles each way to the courthouse. He had a strong tenor voice and on his way home, when he was half a mile away, he would begin singing "La Marseillaise" so the family could hear him and have a hot supper on the table when he arrived. In spite of being a loyal Democrat, in 1840 Pierre campaigned for President William Henry Harrison, giving stump speeches and singing popular political songs. For many years he served as Wayne County commissioner of roads. When Schoolcraft Road was made a corduroy road he donated the logs required to pave it the entire length of their farm.[39] Over the years he became friends with Stevens T. Mason, the first governor of

Michigan, and Henry R. Schoolcraft, a noted Michigan ethnologist, author, and explorer for whom the road was named.

In his spare time, Pierre read law and medicine. Consequently he became an advisor on legal matters to the old pioneer families near him, a service he provided pro bono. He would rest in his garden under the shade of the trees, and neighbors would come by and visit with him. Always proud of his garden, created with such hard work, Pierre worked it and kept it weedless until he was ninety.

Pierre and Angelique remained on the farm until September 1904 when they moved to Detroit to live with a son, Theophilus. In November Pierre walked to the polling booth and voted for Theodore Roosevelt, who he added was "the better candidate." He took his first automobile ride around Belle Isle at ninety-seven.

Of their eight children all but one became teachers. Eugenie Mettetal School in Detroit is named after a daughter whose entire career was spent in the Detroit school system. Emil at eighteen enlisted in the Twenty-fourth Regiment of the Michigan Guards during the Civil War. He survived Andersonville Prison, but at the end of the war the ship returning him home struck a mine off the Carolina coast and everyone onboard was lost. Another son, Eli, was a teacher for thirty-nine years but returned to his agricultural roots when he retired to operate a greenhouse. Pierre and Angelique are commemorated with Mettetal Avenue in Detroit.[40]

Blending education and agriculture was Alsatian-born Leo M. Geismar (1853-1929), who immigrated to the United States in 1879. Seven years later he married Michigan-born Johanna with whom he went on to raise four children.

Geismar and his wife went to the Upper Peninsula in 1887, where they settled in the mining community of Ontonagon. From the beginning he was disposed toward the idea that large undeveloped areas of the Upper Peninsula could be developed as agricultural land. When Michigan Agricultural College (modern Michigan State University) opened its agricultural experimental station in Chatham in the central Upper Peninsula in 1899, Geismar was made its first director in the spring of 1900. The state legislature authorized the station because it realized that the climate and soil were different from the rest of the state. The work of the station was to develop improved practices of agriculture and livestock raising tailored to Upper Peninsula

*Michel L'Huillier (1849–1906)
came to the United States in
1871, worked in the forges, and
eventually developed his own
grocery store in Marquette.
His story was typical of many
Frenchmen who settled
Michigan. (Source: Robert
Bordeau)*

conditions. His first experiment was growing sugar beets, which he did
some ten years before there was any public talk of developing the sugar beet
industry, and well before Michigan's first sugar beet factory was built in 1910.
He went on to experiment with peas, potatoes, and strawberries. Later he
found a strain of corn that was compatible with the Upper Peninsula climate.
His work greatly improved what Upper Peninsula farmers could produce. In
March 1912 he was made agricultural extension expert for the Upper Peninsula, but he refused the position because of the extensive travel involved.
Two years later he became the first agricultural agent in Houghton County,
a position he maintained over the years. Geismar was the founding father of
agronomy in the Upper Peninsula and "one of the foremost agronomists in
Michigan." In 1920 he published *The Upper Peninsula of Michigan* in which
he promoted farming in the region. He was honored by four hundred Upper
Peninsula farmers and spouses who attended his burial in Chatham.[41]

Over the years there were many French immigrants who were farmers
and businessmen and found time to devote to public service. Frederick J.
Barbier was appointed justice of the peace and went on to become county
collector and deputy sheriff. Another, Christopher Damitor in Hamtramck,
served as treasurer, clerk, and supervisor of the city but eventually returned

The L'Huillier family (Georgianna, Marie, and Michel) in 1883 on a trip to Montreal to visit Georgianna's family. (Source: Robert Bordeau)

to his farm. During the Civil War many young French immigrants served in the Union Army like Pierre G. Guilloz who joined the Second Michigan Infantry in 1862.

Cultural Traditions

The French established Catholic churches in various locations throughout Michigan beginning with the Jesuit missionaries. The first Catholic church

The L'Huillier family: Michel, Marie, Clara, and Georgianna in Marquette, Michigan. (Source: Robert Bordeau)

in Detroit—Ste. Anne—was founded in 1701, served the French Canadians and French immigrants, and was considered the "French" church especially to the Irish and Germans. In June 1875, St. Joachim's Catholic Church was established in Detroit and later was expanded due to the growing congregation. After that all French Catholics living east of Woodward Avenue to Connor's Creek would attend St. Joachim's, and those living west of Woodward attended Ste. Anne's. In the late nineteenth century six hundred families belonged to St. Joachim's and eight hundred to Ste. Anne's. In the nineteenth century the first Catholic churches in most communities were established for the French-speaking population and were found throughout the state.

In the early days, until around 1825, following French religious tradition, public processions usually associated with Pentecost and Corpus Christi went from Ste. Anne's to one of the small chapels on the Campau, Lafontaine, or Godfroy farms west of Detroit and to other shrines erected along the route.

In an interesting development in this traditionally Catholic society, the First French Baptist Church was organized on September 20, 1857. The church was erected in May 1861, and in 1864, Reverend Romauld des Roches and Sexton Louis La Racine ministered to a congregation of sixty members. By 1910 the church had been moved to Kerchival and Canton Streets, and Reverend Paul N. Cayar was pastor. Around the time of World War I this French Baptist church ended its existence as membership declined and congregants joined other Baptist churches.

A small number of the descendants of French Huguenots entered Michigan during this century. However, they entered ethnic shadows with their Anglicized names and membership in Protestant churches.

Education

French immigrants have played important roles in the development of education in Michigan. The first educators were the Jesuit missionaries, who established rudimentary schools to educate Native American, métis, and French children. They were followed by Father Gabriel Richard, who in addition to his tenure as a congressman introduced printing and publishing to the state and in 1817 cofounded the University of Michigan. In the nineteenth and twentieth centuries, French Catholic sisters from a variety of religious orders developed schools and other institutions in many areas of the state.

Throughout the nineteenth and twentieth centuries French immigrants, many of them women, were teachers in both private religious and public schools. Many of them taught French, but others taught a variety of subjects.

Both Ste. Anne's and St. Joachim's parishes had their own schools. St. Joachim's parochial school was taught by the Canadian Sisters of the Holy Names of Jesus and Mary of Hochelaga. French parochial schools were found throughout Michigan where a substantial French Canadian population was located.

Folk Tradition

The original French settlers in the Americas brought with them oral traditions that included songs, folktales, legends, and beliefs.[42] A study of French Canadian folklore shows that these Old World forms made their way to Michigan, some having arrived directly from Louis XIV's France in the seventeenth century, others having been colored by first passing through the French Canadian experience. Concerning the study of the French folk tradition, folklorist Richard Dorson pointed out that in Canada "tales are as French as those of the old Provinces of France herself and often in a better state of preservation" and thus "they are of primordial interest for the study of the tale in France proper."[43]

French Catholics had a common body of stories about mythical creatures. The *lutins* are fairy-like creatures found in French folklore and are the only widespread example found in the New World. The *Nain Rouge* is presented as a small child-like creature with blazing eyes, rotten teeth, and red or black boots. The *Nain* could presage terrible events for the day. *Dames blanches* (white women) were female spirits from Lorraine and Normandy who would invite the passerby to dance with them in order to pass by the road. If their invitation was rejected you would be thrown into thistles or briars. *Reynard* (the Fox) originated from Alsace-Lorraine, where many Frenchmen in the United States were from, and played a major role in French folk stories usually making the aristocrats and clergy the butt of his actions.

Fearful superstitions include common elements: transformations, black Bibles, visits of the devil, and evil means of death. One of the most interesting was the loup-garou (a type of werewolf) where a human could change into an animal form at will. There were stories of a loup-garou turning into a hog and the farmer hit the hog in the head only to see his friend the next day with a bandaged head. Another superstition was the appearance of a black dog at your doorstep, which meant someone in the household was going to die. If a nun dressed in her black habit was suddenly encountered, this was a sign of bad luck.

Many of the French farmers brought with them folklore concepts related to planting. Depending on the rising or falling moon what was planted might prosper or do poorly. Potatoes thus should be planted on the falling moon so that they would grow into the ground, for example.

Societies and Organizations

During the nineteenth century a number of French organizations developed in Detroit. A Michigan territorial judge in Detroit, Augustus Woodward in July 1818 wrote a constitution for the "French Moral and Benevolent Society of the City of Detroit and Its Vicinity." Little is known of this society except that Woodward was its first secretary. The Lafayette Benevolent Society was founded in 1853 and incorporated two years later. These and other societies were created for friendship and interaction of the immigrants, and monthly fees provided sick and death benefits. In September 1857 the society planned to raise funds for a "colossal" twenty-four-foot statue of the Revolutionary War hero Gilbert du Motier, the Marquis de Lafayette, to be located in Grand Circus. In order to raise money for the enterprise they promoted excursions on the steamer *Mississippi* on the Detroit River. Unfortunately funding was not enough and the statue was never constructed. By 1868 the society was meeting in its own quarters—Lafayette Hall on Gratiot Street. Two years later, a small branch was established in Bay City. In 1925 and 1926, the Detroit group was meeting in St. Joachim school hall and disbanded soon after. The French Democratic Club was operating in the fall of 1868 as a politically active organization. The group was largely French Canadian in its membership, but attracted some native-born Frenchmen. At the same time there was a group called the Detroit Frenchmen who remained loyal to the memory of Napoleon.[44] In Detroit and throughout the towns and cities of Michigan the French Canadians had a myriad of societies that accepted French-born members.

The French in Detroit were concerned with maintaining their French language. In 1855 French was taught in evening classes.[45] In 1874 Frenchmen and French Canadians met to discuss how best to ensure that French language instruction would be maintained in the public schools. They decided to contact the board of education about their concerns. That same year, the French Cosmopolitan Institute was established with the purpose of preserving the French language through a reading room and French school. Within three months the institute had 160 members from both sides of the Detroit River. Its constitution held that nothing of a sectarian or political nature would be brought before the group and that it was not to be a beneficial society in which members were given financial benefits. As with many of these organizations, it is hard to tell what the eventual outcome of the institute's work was.[46]

As the twentieth century progressed and the French immigrants assimilated into American life, these organizations were no longer needed. During the decade of the 1920s many of these clubs, except the institute, fell victim to these changes in lifestyles. This development was common to other ethnic groups as well.

Newspapers

For the French in Michigan, as with most ethnic communities, the native-language newspaper was an important means of getting information about the Old Country, the ethnic community, and national and foreign news. Also found on the pages of these newspapers were serialized French stories, biographies of famous Frenchmen in North America, and religious items. The newspapers were an important link pulling the French language community together.

French-language newspapers were published in Michigan throughout the nineteenth and twentieth centuries.[47] Gabriel Richard's *Michigan Essay, or Impartial Observer* was the first, though it only lasted one issue (of August 31, 1809).

At midcentury, L. J. Poulin established the French language journal *Le Citoyen* (The Citizen) in Detroit, which was a political, religious, literary, and family-oriented publication. Its main readership was French Canadian, but it was of interest to French immigrants as well. It covered farming, French affairs, and news from Quebec, Michigan, and throughout the United States.[48] This journal lasted just twenty-six issues, published from early 1850 through November 11, 1850.

L'Impartial was published in 1869–70. Between 1889 and 1891 the weekly *L'Union Franco Americain* came along for a short run. The most successful newspaper was *Le Courier du Michigan*, which started publication in Lake Linden in the Copper Country in 1912 and then moved seven years later to Detroit. The paper's dedicated editor, Pierre-Eudore Mayrand, carried on publishing the paper until 1957 when the era of French-language newspapers came to an end.

French Consul

As the French immigrant population stabilized and to honor the centennial of the French Revolution, in 1889 French President Marie François Sadi Carnot appointed Joseph Belanger (1848–1928), a French Canadian, the first French consul to Detroit.[49] Raised and educated in Quebec, Belanger graduated with honors from the Military College of Quebec and studied law before he immigrated to Detroit in 1868. He entered the insurance and real-estate business and became one of the earliest members of the Detroit Board of Commerce. In 1873 he married Madeline Askin Pettier, a member of a pioneer French family. A community spirit, Belanger was a member of numerous religious and social organizations and was an ardent supporter of the Little Sisters of the Poor, whose ministry dealt with the elderly.

Belanger aided French immigrants who needed an official to deal with business, financial, and real-estate problems that arose in France. He was a fine representative of the French government and was the only member of the Detroit consular corps to appear on state occasions in full uniform. With his white trousers, blue dress coat, cocked hat, snow-white sideburns, gold braid, medals, and sword he cut a fine figure.

Over the years he was decorated for his work by the American, French, and Canadian governments. He was decorated by several French educational institutions and was an honorary member of Parisian literary and dramatic societies. In 1927 the French government decorated him with the Legion of Honor, a medal of great prestige. Belanger impressed his contemporaries with his love of French culture, scientific thinking, and wide interest in national and international affairs.

French Observers of and Visitors to Michigan

There were Frenchmen who came as observers of American life and mores and left their mark. In 1831 the noted French political scientist, historian, and social critic Alexis de Tocqueville (1805–59) visited Michigan while on a tour of the United States. Tocqueville had entered the service of the French government by choice, but after the July Revolution of 1830 he was in a precarious position because of his family ties with the ousted king.

He and a coworker, Gustave Auguste de la Boninière de Beaumont (1802–66), took the opportunity to undertake a nine-month study trip of the United States in order to observe the American prison system. Along the way they collected material that would serve as the basis for Tocqueville's best-known work, *Democracy in America* (1835–40). This is a highly perceptive and prescient analysis of the political and social system of the United States and of the vitality, excesses, and potential future of democracy, with attention to the situation in France. Beaumont wrote a novel, *Marie; or, Slavery in the United States* (2 vols., 1835).

Tocqueville and Beaumont traveled in Michigan for two weeks. On July 19, 1831, the duo boarded a steamboat at Buffalo for Detroit in order to study a frontier community, Saginaw. There Tocqueville tested an idea about the evolution of society from simple to more complex forms by observing and discussing life with residents. Tocqueville wrote about the pioneers they encountered in Michigan, the Native Americans, the French Canadians, and the environment they traveled through. In Detroit Tocqueville interviewed Father Richard about his insights into American politics. In August Tocqueville and Beaumont took the *Superior* and traveled to Sault Ste. Marie and Mackinac Island. On this trip Beaumont wrote of the beauty of the Michigan shoreline. They took a canoe to view the great expanse of Lake Superior and descended through the roaring rapids of the St. Mary's River, which was a travel experience for most tourists to the site.

The pair returned to France in the spring of 1832 and reentered political life. Tocqueville's Michigan essay, *Quinze Jours au Désert* (A Fortnight in the Wilderness), was published posthumously in Paris nearly three decades later, in 1860. The work discusses the role of the Indians on the frontier along with the spread of democratic society. Tocqueville saw at Saginaw on the fringes of civilization a similar society as he had seen elsewhere. At Sault Ste. Marie he encountered the blending of Indian and French society.[50]

Other notable Frenchmen visited Michigan. Among them was François d'Orléans, Prince Joinville, the son of King Louis Phillipe, who traveled through the Great Lakes in the summer of 1841 and briefly visited Mackinac Island and saw the sights. A story recounted by Reverend Eleazer Williams of Green Bay was that the prince had revealed to him that Williams was the "lost Dauphin" or Louis XVII, although it is most likely that the dauphin had died in prison.[51]

The prominent paleontologist Philippe Édouard Poulletier de Verneuil (1805–73) traveled throughout Europe studying fossils. In 1846 he came to the United States and studied the paleological period of fossils in New York, Pennsylvania, Ohio, and Indiana, examining the connection between the fossils of North America and Europe. Before his return to France in October he visited the Copper Country, observing the developing copper mines but not focusing on fossil remains. Later he presented his findings on North American geology.[52]

The mining engineer Louis-Édouard Rivot visited Michigan and the Upper Peninsula to learn about the potential of copper deposits there in the 1850s. He is the subject of more discussion later in the story.

In the summer of 1861, Prince Napoleon, who was the cousin of Napoleon III and the son of Jérôme Napoléon (brother of Napoleon I), and his wife Princess Clotide came to the United Sates on a personal trip, accompanied by an entourage of friends and attendants. An important member of this party was Lieutenant-Colonel Camille Ferri Pisani, the prince's second aide-de-camp. During the trip he wrote letters to his superior, Colonel Franconière in Paris. These are a source of insights into the French perspective on American life, mores, and the environment and a useful description of Michigan and its people.[53]

Twentieth Century and Beyond

The opening of the twentieth century showed that French immigration to Michigan continued to show signs of stagnation. As in the previous century, the relatively small numbers of French immigrants were found throughout the state, with goodly numbers even living in the Upper Peninsula. However the largest number were concentrated along the modern I-75 corridor between Monroe in the south and Bay City in the north, with Wayne County and Detroit continuing to attract the largest number in any Michigan county.

As seen in the nineteenth century, it is difficult to put these French immigrants into any one occupation. The women found employment as dressmakers, servants, and housekeepers. The males became farmers in agrarian counties or worked in the copper and iron mines in the Upper Peninsula; Frenchmen living in St. Charles in Saginaw County were coal miners, while others found employment in service and technological industries and as craftsmen.

France and the Automobile

French immigrants also played an important role in the early automobile industry, the dominant industry in twentieth-century Michigan. Their **45** involvement began before World War I when the automobile industry consisted of many small and large independent manufacturers, with the Ford Motor Company dominating the scene. Although autos were built throughout the southeastern part of the state, Wayne County was the center of this industry. In the spring of 1920 there were an estimated 4,174 French immigrants in Michigan, with over half of them living in Wayne County; of this number, discounting wives, children, and nonworking relatives, there were 409 French immigrants employed in the county. Frenchmen were found as laborers (6.5 percent), in the food services (10 percent), as craftsmen (10 percent), in the technical-industrial sector (20 percent), and finally in the automotive industry (53 percent or 218 workers).

In the automobile industry, French immigrants tended to be hired in areas where technical skills were in demand. Nearly half of them were employed as machinists, with smaller numbers working as tool makers, pattern makers, carpenters, leather workers, welders, tire builders, or simply as laborers. A group of Frenchmen were listed in managerial-level positions, such as engineers, designers, salesmen, superintendents, inspectors, and foremen. This was also true of Frenchmen finding positions in the auto companies in Flint. They held positions as electricians, loaders, laborers, and machinists, and one immigrant was a physician for an auto company. In the Lansing area one was an inspector for a crankshaft factory and another was an assembler in a gas engine factory, all related to the automobile.

Beginning in the late nineteenth century and ending with the rise of Henry Ford and his mass-production methods, France was the world's leading automobile producer. The French had imagination, capital, skilled mechanics, and some of the best roads in the world. In 1905 Ford and his engineers discovered a French-made steel-vanadium alloy that impressed them with its low weight and high strength. Ford used this so-called V-steel in the chassis of the Model T to reduce the car's overall weight to about half that of contemporary automobiles. In the coming years vanadium steel would go on to be used in French luxury cars as well. A Model-T might break down every so often, but it would not fall apart.

The two dominant French automobile manufacturers, Louis Renault and later André-Gustave Citroën, viewed the Ford experience as worthy of study. Renault started his automobile company in 1898. In 1912, as sales of European automobiles declined, Renault decided to visit Ford. Renault knew that he could compete with the Ford factories building the Model-T to regain the market share. Ford and Renault were similar in many ways, beginning with the fact that both men built their firms from nothing. Ford regarded Renault as one of the few foreign manufacturers on his level. The two men hit it off well and spent hours over the drawing board studying models and blueprints, communicating through sign language in the absence of an interpreter. When Renault returned to France he and other French manufacturers realized that they must modernize or watch the expanding automobile market fall to the Americans. He borrowed from Ford the "vertical concentration of industry" so that his plants would not have to be dependent on other sources of materials.[54]

The other major French auto manufacturer was André-Gustave Citroën who invented the double helical gear and in 1906 became the successful director of Mors Motor Company in Paris.[55] In 1912 Citroën came to the United States, visited with Ford, and became "Fordized." He returned to France overflowing with ideas. He was fascinated with Ford's mass-production methods, which involved well-lit halls on a single floor. He used these principles for making shells for France during World War I. Another was the notion of producing one model that, like the Model-T, would be a light, popular car made inexpensive by mass production. The Citroën Model A came out in May 1919 as the first inexpensive European automobile. Citroën also adopted Ford's management lead in providing social service for his workers. Thus the automobile companies and their owners on both sides of the Atlantic interacted to help each other in addition to competing. Citroën (1998) and Renault (2003), along with Armand Peugeot (1999), have been inducted into the Automotive Hall of Fame in Dearborn.

In Michigan a few French immigrants or their sons played major roles in the development of the automobile industry. The most famous of these was Louis Joseph Chevrolet (1878–1941), who was born in Switzerland but raised in France. In his youth, Chevrolet built a wine pump for filling wine vats with juice from the grape press, worked on bicycles, and became a successful racing cyclist. It was an easy move from the world of bicycles to cars, and starting in 1896 he worked for a series of automakers.

In 1900 Chevrolet came to the United States by way of Canada. He worked for a time as a chauffeur, as a salesman for a number of European automobile companies, and then as an auto racer. In 1905 he married Suzanne Treyvoux.

In 1907 Chevrolet met William C. Durant, the founder of General Motors, and Durant recognized the young mechanic's ability and hired him. Chevrolet created innovations that spurred the Buick racing team for years. As a result of this activity the Chevrolet Motor Company was formed, and Chevrolet sold his name to Durant. The first Chevrolet Classic 6 was big, powerful, and expensive at $2,150, but Durant needed a cheaper high-volume car for the American market. Without informing Chevrolet, Durant created a smaller four-cylinder car, the Model H. Chevrolet was not happy with this development and disassociated himself with Durant. Little did he know that the Chevrolet brand would sell over 125 million cars and become an icon in the American auto world.

Chevrolet left the company and sold his low-valued stock. If he had kept the stock, he would have become a millionaire. In 1916 he and his brothers, Gaston and Arthur, both immigrants, organized the Frontenac Motor Corporation, named after the illustrious governor of New France. The company built four- and eight-cylinder models, and Chevrolet raced them with his brother Gaston. Although the company was not a success, going out of business in 1923, Chevrolet said he was prouder of these racers than all of the Chevrolets being produced. Louis Chevrolet is memorialized at the entrance to the Indianapolis Motor Speedway Hall of Fame Museum and has been inducted into numerous halls of fame.

French-born Gaston Chevrolet (1892–1920) was a Michigan auto manufacturer and developed into a racecar champion driver. In the 1920 Indianapolis 500 driving a Monroe-Frontenac he came in first place, thus breaking the dominance of European-built cars. He also became the first driver in the history of the race to go the distance without making a tire change. In November 1920 he was killed in a race at the Beverly Hills Speedway in California, but despite the crash had accumulated enough points during the race and season to win the 1920 title of "Speed King of the Year" (the AAA National Champion). In 2002 he was inducted into the Motorsports Hall of Fame of America.[56]

French Nomenclature

In the 1910s Americans increasingly dominated the automobile industry and found themselves with a nomenclature dilemma. It was necessary either to borrow words from the French or to create words in English, and the former was an easier route to go. The American language was immediately enriched by a long list of French words, which quickly became part of the daily lexicon.[57]

The basic word "automobile" came about in 1886 with the invention of a self-propelled vehicle used to carry passengers. The carburetor used to mix air and fuel was an Italian invention in 1876, but the French word *carbure*, "to combine with carbon," became the basis for this word. In French the word *chauffeur* means "fireman" or "stoker." The early cars were steamers and required two men to operate them, the *mécanicien* and the *chauffeur*—the mechanic and the fireman. The word entered the English language in 1899 and acquired a specific definition as a paid driver of an automobile. In 1917 the verb "to chauffeur" also entered the language. "Chassis" means a "frame" and refers to the frame of the automobile. The word "garage," which entered the English language in 1902, means a railroad siding in French, but as applied to automobiles means a room or building where cars are kept ready for use.

The French *tonneau* or "tone" came from the Old French word *tonnel* or "cask" and entered the English language in 1901. Today a tonneau cover protects unoccupied passenger seats in a convertible or roadster, or the bed of a pickup truck.

The word "limousine" has the most picturesque origin of all. A *Limousine* is a woman who lives near the city of Limoges, the capital of the old province of Limousin. The peasant women of this region wore a sort of coif or hood with a cape attached, which also became known as a "limousine." The French developed a covered cart, much like a prairie schooner, that they also called a "limousine." When the closed, weather-proof body of the automobile was devised, what more natural name to call it than a "limousine." This word entered the English language in 1902, and today refers to a luxury automobile with separate compartments for the passengers and driver. In 1968 the abbreviated term "limo" first appeared in the *New Yorker*.

Other French words and definitions entered English. In 1908 the word "coupe" meaning a closed two-door car with two seats, came into use in English. In 1939 the "coupe de ville" was first used referring to a type of automobile with passenger seats that are covered but with a driver's compartment that is either open or optionally covered by a fold down roof. Even "taxicab" was adopted from the French *taxmètre* and put to use in English in 1913.

Besides these terms from the French language, the names of three French explorers in Michigan and one governor were used for naming automobiles. The term Marquette, named after the Jesuit explorer and missionary Jacques Marquette, was used for sets of autos. In 1912 the Marquette Motor Company, controlled by General Motors, built four body types, using forty and forty-five horsepower engines. Between 1929 and 1931 the Buick Motor Company of Flint produced a Marquette model, with prices ranging from $990 for the business coupe to $1,060 for the sedan. It was hoped that this inexpensive auto would weather the Depression, but this was not the case. The Cadillac Motor Car Company of Detroit has been producing the Cadillac since 1903. Both were named for Antoine Cadillac, the founder of Detroit in 1701. The Chevrolets' company, Frontenac Motor Corporation, which was created in 1916 and produced the Frontenac racer, was named after the French governor Louis de Buade, Count de Frontenac. The La Salle, named after the seventeenth-century French explorer René-Robert de La Salle, was also produced between 1927 and 1940 by the Cadillac Motor Car Company, a part of General Motors.

World War I

Life for all immigrants in Michigan had developed into a predictable pattern of life and work. World War I started slowly in the summer of 1914, then grew into a crescendo of violence centered in northern France. Between June 28 and late July, Michiganians read their newspapers and followed the world coming apart with dread and concern. Particularly troubled were the various immigrant groups whose nations would become allies or enemies of the United States during the course of the war. The French immigrants were no exception.

The war pitted the Central Powers—Germany, Austria-Hungary, and Turkey—against the Allied Powers: France, Britain, Russia, Italy, and beginning in 1917, the United States. The declarations of war began on July 28, 1914, when Austria-Hungary declared war on Serbia due to the assassination of Archduke Ferdinand and his wife, Sophie, in Sarajevo. Other nations followed, with Germany and France declaring war on August 3. Many French immigrants heeded the call to return to France and fight for the homeland. Louis Marot, a waiter in the Café Frontenac in Detroit, told a reporter for the

Detroit News that he considered unmarried Frenchmen who did not return to fight for France as traitors and poor Frenchmen. French immigrants looking to return visited the office of French consul Joseph Belanger to put their papers in order.[58] He was their official link with the Old Country. Frenchmen of all walks—waiters, engineers, mechanics—entrained for New York City, paying their own fare to return to France to serve their country.[59] The French liner *Rochambeau* was waiting for them in New York harbor.[60]

On the other hand there were many like Eddie Chartier, who stated to a reporter "naturally, as it should be, my sympathies are with France, but, like the other French people of Detroit, I have been here so long that I am thoroughly Americanized, and, as an American, I remain neutral." He felt that French people in Detroit were not paying a great deal of attention to the war, but that they all agreed it was sad to see so many good men sacrificed by the actions of the rulers.[61]

The calamity of the war dampened the spirits of Detroit's festive cafes. Proprietors feared that French champagnes like Clicquot, Mumm, and Pommery would quickly become scarce and extremely expensive. As one fellow observed "we'll have to be content with the stuff that comes from Milwaukee and the grape factories of California."[62]

Detroit's automobile companies took an immediate interest in the war. Every automobile in the Detroit-based Packard Motor Company branch in Paris was commandeered by the government, and the employees were ordered off to the mobilization camps. As a result the branch was closed for the duration of the war. Many of Detroit's automobile men talked of an increase in American auto sales because European models could not be sent to Latin America and other nations not at war. The Standard Truck Company and other Detroit manufacturers began negotiating with the warring governments for the sale of trucks.

Tragic news from the front in France quickly arrived in Detroit. In 1910 thousands of Detroiters at the state fairgrounds had held their breath in suspense as they watched the airborne antics of aviator Roland Garros. The handsome Frenchman was known personally to many Detroiters. Now on August 4, 1914, they read that Garros coolly went to his death by ramming a huge zeppelin high up in the air, taking with him twenty-five Germans. Ladis Lewkowitz of New York, a member of the Paris Aero Club and a close friend of Garros, was in Detroit visiting the consul. He planned to offer his services to France and commented on the fact that France had five thousand aircraft.

If some people were concerned about returning to their homes or feared the loss of champagne and fine wines, others were interested in learning about the nations in the conflict and following the battles. The Detroit Public Library highlighted in the *Detroit News* and made available books focused on the principal nations including France.[63]

Due to an efficient American propaganda machine operated by the government, anti-German sentiment spread throughout Michigan. The teaching of German, which had ranked as one of the most popular and widely taught foreign languages in the state, was universally abandoned by schools and colleges and replaced by French and Spanish. To honor the 1914 battle of the Marne, where the French blunted the initial German offensive in the west, the little town of Berlin, near Grand Rapids, changed its name to Marne.

Much of the fighting that involved the United States after war was declared in April 1917 took place in France. Michigan furnished 135,485 men to the armed forces during the war, of which approximately 5,000 died in service and another 15,000 were wounded. Many of these men fought on the French front. Michigan's National Guard saw extensive and prolonged service on the European war fronts as part of the Thirty-second or Red Arrow Division. Between January and March 1918 members of the guard arrived in France and remained in combat until the end of the war eight months later. The guard took part in the battle of the Aisne, the Oise-Aisne offensive, and the Meuse-Argonne action, which finally broke the German offensive. Out of 27,000 men serving with the guard, 2,671 men were killed and 10,242 were wounded—high causalities.

In order to prepare Michiganians for their stay in France, the *Detroit News* carried a public service piece during the summer of 1918. They ran a series of twelve language lessons on proper phonetic pronunciation, which would allow the prospective soldier to learn a 1,800-word vocabulary in subsequent weeks.

The automobile plants in southern Michigan slowed auto production and focused on trucks for the war effort. On December 12, 1917, a convoy of trucks from the Packard plant in Detroit were driven to Baltimore for shipment to France. The Reo factory in Lansing produced armored trucks. Pontiac's

French tannery workers enjoying an aperitif at a boarding house saloon. Ethnic saloons allowed immigrants the opportunity to visit, reminisce about the Old Country, and catch up on news of the community. (Source: Russell Magnaghi)

Oakland plant produced tanks, and Packard and several other Michigan plants produced Liberty airplane engines. The Ford Motor Company employed its mass-production techniques to manufacture submarine chasers. Although these products went into the general war effort, most of these items found their way to France where most of the Allied fighting was taking place. In a sense, France, which had created colonial Michigan in the seventeenth century, was now being repaid.

Bastille Day, July 14

The Bastille was a medieval fortress in Paris that became a symbol of despotism. In the seventeenth and eighteenth centuries the Bastille was used as a state prison and a place of detention for important political prisoners. On July 14, 1789, at the opening of the French Revolution, an armed mob of Parisians captured the fortress and released its prisoners. This was a dramatic act that came to symbolize the beginning of the end of the ancien régime. The revolutionary government subsequently demolished the Bastille. Since 1880, Bastille Day (July 14) has been a French national holiday. It is observed in grand style in France and in communities in the United States. However, many French people and French Americans in the United States celebrate the day simply with a rendition of "La Marseillaise" and a picnic or dinner, but the day is celebrated.[64]

Over the years the French in Michigan have celebrated the day in a variety of ways. In 1902 the French American Club held a banquet and games in a beflagged Saint Jean Baptiste Hall at 476 Fort Street in Detroit.[65] In 1918, in the middle of World War I, Detroit citizens came together as a group to celebrate a day of freedom and independence. A grand parade was held to the State Armory in Detroit where the crowd was welcomed by the French consul, Joseph Belanger. This was followed by patriotic speeches of solidarity and flag waving from a variety of nations—the United States, Belgium, and Italy, as well as Poland, Lebanon, Syria, and Czechoslovakia (nations to be after the war). The highly charged patriotic evening concluded with multinational hymns. Detroit came together to pay tribute to France, which "all Europe honors."[66]

In subsequent years less elaborate celebrations were held that were usually focused on the French community. For instance in 1921 Detroiters of French descent, many of them wearing in their coat lapels the Tricolor intertwined with the Stars and Stripes, began the day with a prayer service at St. Joachim Church followed by the Lafayette Society's sponsored outing to Sugar Island in the Detroit River attended by eight hundred. In the evening the various French societies had brief patriotic programs, and the editor of the *Detroit News* editorialized the importance of Bastille Day.[67]

As the years passed Bastille Day seems to have become less important as a city event. In 1937 French groups of war veterans and brides and the French Friendship Club held a dinner and entertainment at the American Legion Home in Detroit. Three years later, after France fell to Germany on June 22, Bastille Day turned out to be a sad day of commemoration. Six hundred people including many French and Belgian war veterans attended the services at St. Joachim's Church.[68]

Since the end of World War II French immigrant and French American interest in Bastille Day has waned and ebbed. However in 2000 the Grosse Pointe Historical Society held a pre-Bastille Day event and promoted the Michigan connection with France and French traditions. It was a way to reconnect with the French heritage of the community.[69]

Postwar Results

Some of the American soldiers who served in France developed romantic interests with local French women, married them, and brought them back to Michigan. An accurate number of French brides is missing. Life for these new immigrants was difficult as they were young, unfamiliar with American society and culture, away from their families, and unable to speak the language. A similar development took place after World War II (discussed below).

During World War I, nations abandoned all industrial development excepting that with the object of winning the war. American mining, however, was not at a standstill during the war, and at the end of the war mining engineers visited the Calumet and Hecla copper mine in Calumet. In October 1919 three French mining engineers arrived to inspect the mining methods of the district. They were quickly followed by a Belgian mine manager and three Japanese mining engineers.

After the war was over in November 1918, there were a number of events that tied French immigrants and others to France. The girl warrior of fifteenth-century France, Joan of Arc, made the news on May 16, 1920, when Pope Benedict XV declared her a saint. There were celebrations throughout France. French immigrants in the United States and Michigan celebrated as well. The French parliament quickly decreed a national festival in Joan of Arc's honor to be held on the second Sunday of every May. Catholics in Michigan could celebrate her feast on May 30. The event was especially piquant because of Joan of Arc's involvement in recovering France from English domination during the Hundred Years' War of the 1400s, which led to the coronation of Charles VI and her death by treachery at nineteen years of age. Today a Catholic parish in St. Clair Shores dedicated to St. Joan of Arc honors this French heroine-saint.

Visit by Marshal Foch

The great hero of World War I was Ferdinand Foch (1851–1929), the commander of the Allied forces and the leader considered most responsible for the Allied victory. After the war he was showered with honors including the honorary title of "marshal of France." He came to the United States in

October 1921 to make a grand tour of the nation, making several stops in Michigan. His liaison officer was Michigan resident Colonel Frank Drake who did business in Paris for many years. Foch arrived in Michigan by rail in early November from Chicago. Throughout his visit he referred to Detroit's foundation "through the wisdom and foresight of my fellow countrymen" and praised the beautiful city of more than a million residents. He went on:

> The courage and determination of its early settlers apparently have been handed down from one generation to another and not only have made Detroit one of the most industrial centers in the world, but also produced those Michigan soldiers whose hardihood and courage in the late war were well known to me.[70]

On November 7 at a stop in Battle Creek to dedicate the new Roosevelt Memorial Hospital he was greeted by thousands of enthusiastic people, Governor Alex J. Groesbeck, and members of the state supreme court. In his welcome Groesbeck said "we of Michigan want him to know America cherishes for him a reverential respect almost equal to that she holds for the memories of Washington and Lincoln and of Roosevelt." At Ann Arbor he was greeted by faculty and students and was unhappy that he could not linger at "the great University of Michigan."[71]

At his arrival in Detroit at the Michigan Central Station he was greeted by thousands of people, Mayor James Cozens, and members of the city's French community. At Dodge Main automobile plant in Hamtramck, the Dodge family and company officials welcomed him, and he was given an abbreviated tour of the plant where munitions for the French .75 cannon had been made during the war. After a long day of freezing temperatures, the seventy year-old general, who looked like a kindly grandfather, was greeted with a standing ovation by five thousand people as he entered the Michigan State Armory. Having led the Allies through the terrible recent war, his last speech of the day stressed the role of peace in the world.

This was his last event in Detroit as he headed for Cleveland. Some four hundred thousand people had witnessed Marshal Foch in the Motor City, the largest crowds on his tour to date. He was praised in newspaper editorials, and the J. L. Hudson department store even welcomed and praised him in an advertisement for "pettibockers" and Gossard corsets for women.

French Clubs

Although a variety of French clubs and benevolent societies had developed in the nineteenth century, others developed in the twentieth century as well. In outlying towns French immigrants could join French-Canadian clubs where the French language was spoken. The main clubs and organizations developed in the Detroit area where the French immigrant population was the largest in the state. On March 3, 1902, delegates met in New York City to establish the Federation des Alliances Françaises whose purposes were to promote French culture and language. A delegate from Detroit was in attendance. Little is known of the alliance's activities, but in the fall of 1919, at the end of World War I, the alliance began an annual cultural lecture program. It was pointed out that in the past the alliance had been a luxury, but now it was a necessity so that strong and permanent bonds could be reestablished between France and the United States in the wake of the war. The speaker for the evening was Madame La Marrone de Marivetz who gave a lecture titled "The Cathedral of Rheims Before and After the Bombardment." Members at the time had access to varied programs, French magazines, a French library, and free French language classes. The Alliance Française was reactivated after World War II, and today alliance branches operate in Bloomfield Hills, Grosse Pointe, Grand Rapids, Kalamazoo, and Lansing. Today the popular and active alliance attracts not only French-born members but many American-born Francophiles to its language classes and cultural programs.

A number of French religious societies were connected with Catholic churches and tended to be centered in Detroit with its large French population. There was St. Joseph's Roman Catholic Benevolent Society, St. Louis de Gonzaga Society, and by 1908, the Société de Ste. Marthe associated with Notre Dame de la Visitation church. There was also an insurance-related group called the Union of Roman Catholic Societies, which operated into the 1920s.

French war brides organized after the war, and in 1933 they named their group the Club of French War Brides in Detroit. Five years later the organization was renamed the French Women's Benevolent Club to reflect a larger outlook, but the basic aims of social interaction and a promotion of Franco-American ties remained. A year later the organization officially obtained its articles of incorporation with the name change.[72]

*Coming from
France, known as
a center of fashion,
immigrants and
their American-born
children dressed up
for Sunday Mass or
to celebrate events
like Bastille Day
(July 14). (Source:
Robert Bordeau)*

During the 1920s two short-lived French clubs existed in Detroit. The Franco-American Club, headquartered at 704 Cadillac Square Building, was active in 1926 and 1927. The France-American Society, located at 404 Donovan Building, came and went soon after. By the early 1930s both of these organizations were no longer found in the city directories.

Since at least the nineteenth century, descendants of French Protestant Huguenots or followers of John Calvin had been settling in Michigan. Some like Mathew Hasbrouck settled in Marshall, Michigan, and others became leading businessmen in Detroit and other cities. The National Huguenot Society was founded in New York City in 1883, and its goals were to inform the public of Huguenot history and persecution in France and settlement in the American colonies, and to perpetuate the religious movement.

The Huguenot Society of Michigan was established on June 22, 1937, in Marshall, Michigan, at the Matthew Hasbrouck House, the home of Mrs. George W. Moran, the organizing president. Michigan became the sixth

state to form a Huguenot Society and to affiliate with the National Huguenot Society. Thirty-five Huguenot descendants from Detroit, Fowlerville,
Grand Rapids, Grosse Pointe, Highland Park, Jackson, Marshall, Tecumseh,
Three Rivers, Tipton, and Toledo, Ohio, met for the day to plan the society's
future. The group's objective was to perpetuate the memory and promote
the principles and virtues of the Huguenots, French Protestants who were
persecuted by Louis XIV in the seventeenth century. Once organized they
celebrated a Day of Remembrance and held an annual meeting.[73] Over the
years the Huguenot Society of Michigan has continued with a low profile,
producing yearbooks into the 1980s.

Other clubs prospered, and in 1939 along with the Alliance Française and
French Women's Benevolent Club there was the Club Amical Française promoting friendship and the French Benevolent Society. During the early days
of World War II when the United States was neutral and France fell to Nazi
Germany, they raised funds for food and clothing for the French Red Cross
through the French Committee for Relief in France. The French Women's
Benevolent Club remained active well into the twentieth century.

French culture and heritage continues to be promoted in Michigan. In
1982 Madame Cadillac Dance Theatre was organized whose purpose is to
highlight French colonial life in Michigan through authentic dance, music,
and costumes. Over the years the group has presented well-received programs throughout the state, especially at the Alliance Française.

During the Great Depression of the 1930s few French immigrants arrived
in Michigan. By the spring of 1940 there were 3,364 French immigrants in
the state that were not recent arrivals. The numbers had not changed much
since the 1860 census. The five counties with around one hundred French
immigrants or more were Wayne (1,953),[74] Oakland (139), Saginaw (121),
Macomb (114), and Genesee (99), which had become traditional centers of
French population.

World War II

During the late 1930s French nationals in Michigan watched and read letters
from friends and relatives in France as European events were being driven to
the brink by Nazi Germany. With the coming of World War II on September
1, 1939, they were stunned by how rapidly the Germans overran France by

June 22, 1940. The country was divided into Nazi-occupied France and Vichy France, a puppet state. This ended with the Allied invasion of North Africa in November 1942 when Hitler annulled the earlier armistice and occupied the whole country.

From the start the French in Michigan received information of the costly and oppressive German occupation of the country, with thousands executed and hundreds of thousands sent to Germany as slave labor. At the same time General Charles de Gaulle proclaimed from London the existence of the "Free French" who now fought with the Allies.

In the beginning the Michigan French organized themselves to aid their stricken countrymen. By mid-July 1940 Germaine de Pons of Birmingham was the general chairwoman of the local chapter of the Committee for French War Relief. Maxime Raingust was the chair for the collection of used clothing to be shipped to the Old Country. Local aid was sent and letters and reports received of the drastic conditions in France. There was little the immigrants could do, although many of their sons and daughters joined the American military once war was declared in December 1941.

French immigrants had to watch the general war news coming from Europe, which offered no specific information about friends and relatives in the Old Country, though some detailed news about France arrived with coverage of D-Day in June 1944. By November French people in Detroit and elsewhere in the state began to receive letters from home, often via Allied soldiers who brought them to the United Kingdom and then to the United States. They read about the devastation of homes and businesses at Le Havre and other cities in Normandy, as well as wartime stories. This war proved to be much different from World War I when France was not invaded but the war fought at its margins.

French War Brides

Both world wars brought thousands of American men to France, where some naturally met their future wives.[75] After the war many Michigan servicemen returned home with war brides, many of whom were eager to bid adieu to wartime France and its reality of disrupted life, shortages of food and goods, oppressive enemy occupation, terror, and death. On the positive side for these young, and in some cases naive, women was the romance and excitement of meeting a young American serviceman in a military uniform. Brief romances occasionally led to marriages, which were not always encouraged by the U.S. Army. Many of these war brides came to the United States and remained, often for years, without acquiring any official immigration status or recognition from the federal government. They were essentially illegal immigrants after World War II. By 1945, there were so many war brides in this situation that the U.S. Congress passed a federal law, the War Brides Act, authorizing the admission of the wives and children of citizens serving in the American armed forces during the war without regard to quotas or other standards.

The excitement of romance and the anticipation of a new life in America often masked the reality these women faced upon arrival. Life for the newly arrived war brides was markedly different from life in wartorn France. They were away from their traditional surroundings, homes, families, and friends. New friendships would have to be made, but before that could happen, they would have to deal with a new language. Then there were the in-laws who might have varying views and attitudes toward these French women their sons planned to marry or had married. There was the role of religion as most of these French women were Catholic and now they would learn that possibly their in-laws were Protestant or Jewish.

War brides settled primarily in Metropolitan Detroit and Grand Rapids, but also in small communities throughout the state. Life in the cities could include other French residents. There were special language and orientation classes. However, in the late 1940s many women in the United States were isolated in their homes, and this isolation was all the more profound for immigrants living in a new and foreign environment. Radios and movies provided an outlet to the external world, and some of them used these means to improve their language skills. The telephone was the means of encountering and communicating with other war brides who were struggling with assimilating into American life and society. The French Women's Benevolent Club was an important social outlet for these women, as stated earlier. Its aims were to preserve friendship among the women, promote the moral and social interest of everyone, and cultivate a spirit of loyalty toward the United States and devotion toward France. The women felt that though they were expatriates and loved their new homeland they were not going to forget their country of origin.

Unfortunately despite their own and outside best efforts, some of these young women could not cope with the difficult transition. Being unable to deal with their new environment and finding that their husbands were not what they seemed to be led to divorce and further alienation in this new land. Unable to deal with the situation, some went the route of new careers or returned to France.

Contemporary French Presence

After the war, France rebuilt and there was even less reason to leave, but French culture and industry entered Michigan especially Metropolitan Detroit. In the spring and summer of 1949 a group of Frenchmen called "The Marquette Team" entered Canada and came to the United States, retracing the Marquette-Joliet voyage from St. Ignace through the Mississippi Valley in 1673. Interest in French culture continued, and since the late 1950s the Cine Club Français de Detroit meets frequently at the Detroit Institute of Arts to view and discuss French movies. During this same period French companies promoted French clothing, wines, and cheeses as they entered the American market through promotion by the consul in Detroit.

Given the industrial nature of the Michigan economy and the role of the automobile industry, in the early years of the twenty-first century, French business interests continue to be involved in the state and to bring in an expatriated labor force. The Michigan chapter of the French-American Chamber of Commerce actively promotes French business in the state. Its work has paid off; glass and window manufacturer Saint-Gobain Sekurit, USA, opened their first North American plant in Shelby Township in 2001. Other French companies include Peugeot-Citroën; Sanofi-Aventis U.S., an international pharmaceutical company headquartered in Rochester Hills; Dassault Systèmes, providing computer software development and programming as well as architectural and engineering services through offices in Troy, Auburn Hills, and Northville; and Plastic Omnium, to highlight a few. French companies in Michigan operate in such varied fields as automobiles, aerospace, retail, luxury goods, furniture, food and wine, agriculture, technology, and medical products. In 2009 there were more than 160 French companies operating in Michigan, with most of them located in Oakland County.

They came to the state because of its favorable location, skilled workforce, affordable cost of living, and direct flights to France, China, and virtually all important commercial centers. Furthermore, the Michigan Economic Development Corporation has lured French businesses with tax incentives.

Partly as a result of these business connections, there are over two thousand French expatriates in Michigan, with some 90 percent living in Metropolitan Detroit. As a result the French School of Detroit has developed, and it serves transplants and provides families with academic and social opportunities. Working with the Birmingham public schools, the French School educates the children in French and English and gives them the opportunity to learn about American culture and language while retaining their native French studies. The Alliance Française provides a similar service to these expatriates. Besides these recent French immigrants or temporary transplants, scattered throughout Michigan are numerous former French students who stayed in Michigan after graduating and married local spouses.

Life for the French expatriate is a process of assimilating into American life, thought, and language. They have to maneuver between two cultures. Everything from shopping to dining has to be relearned in the United States and ultimately the way the peoples of the two cultures think about life. Many of these expatriates maintain elements of French culture like celebrating Christmas gift giving on January 6, making and serving crepes on Mardi Gras at the onset of Lent, and remembering Bastille Day with a dinner or picnic. Some of them, though knowing that they will return to France in a few years, make annual trips home to visit family and friends. All of them make a strong effort to maintain their cultural ties by attending French cultural events.

French culture, which expatriates enjoy and Americans want to share with them, is alive and well in Michigan, thanks to the programs of the French consulate office in Chicago. The Alliance Française is a useful organization teaching the French language and promoting French culture and attracts many expatriates. The French language is heard on Michigan television via Canadian television on Detroit's Channel 54-CBEF-TV and on the radio on CBEF (540 AM), a French-Canadian station outside of Quebec.

An outstanding French immigrant to the world of the automobile is François Castaing who was born in Marseille in 1945 and graduated in engineering from École Nationale Supérieure d'Arts et Métiers in Paris. He worked his way into Renault, and in 1980 he and his family moved to Detroit. He then played a leading role in the development of American Motors and Chrysler and is known for product lifecycle management and an automobile platform team approach. He oversaw the development of the Dodge Intrepid, Jeep Grand Cherokee, and Dodge Viper. Castaing has been elected to the Automotive Hall of Fame.

One of the outstanding developments to take place in Detroit was the resurgence of the Detroit Symphony Orchestra under French conductor, organist, and composer Paul Paray (1886–1979). During his eleven-year tenure (1951–62) as conductor he molded the orchestra into the first French orchestra of the United States focusing on French masters.[76] Paray made his most beautiful recordings in Detroit, aided by the new "Living Presence" technique of Mercury Records, some of which are available in digital form. He was made an honorary citizen of Detroit, and the French government awarded him its highest honor, the Grand-Croix de la Légion d'honneur, in 1975.

French cuisine is found throughout Metropolitan Detroit and other cities in southern Michigan. The most iconic French restaurant was the 1913 Room in the Amway Grand Hotel in Grand Rapids where well-dressed servers delivered such classic French-influenced entrees as dover sole meunière to tables decked out with rich linens and custom glass and silverware surrounded by Louis XIV décor. In 2002 it was awarded the AAA Five Diamond rating, the first and only one in Michigan, which it maintained for ten years. An important part to this fine restaurant was its fastidious French maître d' Denis Cerezo, who maintained high standards. Unfortunately it closed in 2011 due to changing customer dining habits. Even on the Northern Michigan University campus in Marquette, outstanding, high-quality food service and menus were introduced by Madagascar born, French raised Chef André Maile until his departure in 2007. French Canadian Jim Lark owns and serves as maître d' of The Lark in West Bloomfield, a high-end French restaurant that has been consistently recognized with awards and is a favorite with expatriates. In northern Michigan at Traverse City Guillaume Hazael-Massieux, a native of France, operates two outstanding restaurants—Le Becasse and Bistro Foufou—combining French atmosphere and cuisine. Thus the French tradition of fine cuisine continues in Michigan.

U.S. and Michigan relations with France are usually warm, though they can get frosty. May 2002 was a warm time, though. That's when the French consul general, Dominique Decherf, presented "Thank You America" certificates to Michigan veterans who had participated in the liberation of France at the end of World War II. More than eight hundred Michigan veterans applied for this honor and were invited to the ceremonies. The Michigan Department of Military and Veterans Affairs hosted the presentations at the Grand Rapids Home for Veterans and later at Michigan State University's auditorium.

If conditions were warm then, by the following winter they grew frosty. In mid-February 2003 the French government took a strong position against becoming involved with the United Nations in a war with Iraq. When the French under President Marc Chirac cautioned against war and basically said "non" to the United States, many Americans lashed out against the French and anything French. On the national level, syndicated columnist George Will berated the French for their anti–Iraq War stand and concluded that the French would soon be inconsequential.[77] The *Detroit Free Press* chronicled a number of nasty incidents against the French in the state. One French teacher received insulting e-mails, questioning her Americanism because she enjoyed French bread rather than soft and tasteless American bread; deliverymen were upset when they had to deliver to a French office; and to the east, in the congressional dining room in Washington, "French fries" informally became "Freedom fries," and a few Michigan restaurants followed this lead. However, even in the midst of this anger, the quality of French culture remained in high regard, and numerous Michiganians continued to travel to Paris to enjoy the art, culture, and food. French wines and champagne continued to be served.

French Legacy

The French legacy in the state can be seen in many areas. One is in the fifty-plus French place names that appear on Michigan maps, especially along river- and lakeshores where early French arrivals frequently passed or settled. These do not include terms that have been Americanized, such as Rivère de Morts, to the Dead River, in Marquette. There are also names of communities with descriptors: Detroit (Narrows), the Grosse Pointes (Large Point), L'Anse (Meadow); Jesuit missionaries: Charlevoix, Allouez, Marquette; and saints: St. Ignace (St. Ignatius founder of the Jesuit order) and Sault Ste. Marie (Falls of the St. Mary's). At the tip of the Keweenaw

Peninsula is the stand of virgin white pines, one of two in the state, named Estivant Pines after the nineteenth-century French owner.

A number of schools in the state, both secular and religious, have been named after prominent Frenchmen. Gabriel Richard Elementary School of Grosse Pointe was opened in the 1920s, about the same time Foch School was opened in Detroit honoring the French general.

Father Gabriel Richard High School in Ann Arbor was founded in 1868 as St. Thomas Parish High School and was renamed in the 1970s when it became a regional high school. There is a Gabriel Richard Elementary School and a separate high school operated by the Archdiocese of Detroit. In St. Clair Shores the French Jesuit martyr is honored by St. Isaac Jogues Elementary School, and in Sault Ste. Marie there is the parish of the North American Martyrs. Father Marquette is honored with a Catholic Central School in Marquette.

This sojourn through French history and development in Michigan is one of many parts. Although the number of French immigrants never rivaled the numbers of Poles or Dutch or Finns in the state, the smaller number of French immigrants who came played important roles in the development of the state. In this case it was not quantity but quality that has made the French different and unique in Michigan for nearly four centuries.

Appendix 1

Cultural Resources

Archives of the Archdiocese of Detroit, 1234 Washington Blvd., Detroit, Michigan 48228-4875; (313) 237-5846; archives@aod.org. Resources: Variety of records from the earliest days of Detroit. Photographic collection. Contact for specific questions.

The Bentley Historical Library, University of Michigan, 1150 Beal Ave., Ann Arbor, Michigan 48109-3482; (734) 764-3482; FAX (734) 936-1333; www. umich.edu/-bhl/. Resources: Collection contains information on individual French settlers and educators especially connected with the University of Michigan.

The Burton Historical Collection, Detroit Public Library, 5201 Woodward Ave., Detroit, MI 48202; (313) 833-1486; detroit.lib.mi.us/burton/index. htm. Resources: City directories, newspaper clippings, obituaries, photographs. The Archdiocese of Detroit has provided the Burton with church records from 1701 to 1900 on microfilm.

Diocese of Marquette, Archives, 347 Rock St., Marquette, Michigan 49855; (906) 227-9117. Resources: Catholic directories, biographies, and photographs of French priests assigned to the diocese.

French Cultural Services, 737 Michigan Avenue South, Suite 1170, Chicago, Illinois 60611; (312) 664-3525; FAX 312-664-9528; general e-mail: mail@consulfrance-chicago.org; cultural department: culture@

consulfrance-chicago.org; education/linguistic department: education@ consulfrance-chicago.org. Resources: This service provides a wealth of information on French culture (film, music, exhibitions, theater, special invitation programs, university exchange programs, grants and scholarships).

French Institute of Michigan, 7100 Lindemere Circle, Bloomfield Hills, Michigan 48301; (248) 538-5440; FAX 248-538-5438; e-mail: michigan@afusa. org. Resources: Also known as Alliance Française, founded in 1893 in Paris where it is headquartered; dedicated to fostering friendly relations between the French and American people, developing the knowledge of the culture of France, encouraging and furthering the study of the French language.

French Trade Commission, 525 Big Beaver Rd., Ste. 202, Troy, Michigan 48083; detroit@dree.org. Resources: The Commission provides information on selling to and investing in France.

The Library of Michigan, 702 W. Kalamazoo St., Lansing, MI 48915; librarian@michigan.gov; http://www.michigan.gov/libraryofmichigan. Resources: Variety of printed material, directories, county histories, census data, largest collection of state newspapers, and the Michigan Collection.

Walter P. Reuther Library, Wayne State University, 5401 Cass Ave., Detroit, Michigan 48202; (313) 577-4024; reutherreference@wayne.edu. Resources: In their vast collection dealing with labor and urban affairs the library has archival material on the French and a wealth of photographs. It is best to call for an appointment.

French Recipes

The following recipes are from southern France from the kitchen of Catherine Claverie Mendiara.

Cod and Olive Oil (*Morue de Huile d'Olive*)

This was a traditional Lenten and Friday dish in France and the reason why French and other fishermen sailed to the Grand Banks of Newfoundland.

Purchase salted cod found in small boxes in your grocery freezer. The salted cod must be rinsed and then set in a bowl of water covering it. Change the water 3-4 times in 8 hours. Fill a large pot with water and bring to a boil. Add the rinsed codfish and cook for 15-20 minutes. Remove from water and flake into a separate bowl. Sprinkle with olive oil and finely chopped garlic and parsley to taste. Add a dozen boiled new potatoes and three hard-boiled eggs. Serve chilled.

Frog Legs (*Cuisses de Grenouilles*)

Prepare as many frog legs as needed. Marinate for several hours or overnight in white wine. Fry in butter until brown. Sprinkle with parsley and serve with lemon quarters or with garlic melted butter.

Pumpkin Soup (*Soupe de Citrouille*)

Pumpkin soup was a peasant favorite in southern France.

Rub olive oil on a small whole pumpkin along with ginger, salt and pepper, and sprigs of fresh thyme or sprinkle with dried thyme. Bake in a 375°F oven until soft. Let it cool and then cut into slices, removing the skin. Now cut into smaller pieces and place in a blender and put on grind. When done add chicken stock depending on the size of the pumpkin. Heat and it is ready to serve.

Crêpes

These are traditionally made at Mardi Gras.

2–3 Tbsp. whole anise	2 cups flour
Few pieces of orange peel	7 or more eggs
1 cup milk	1 ladle (⅓ cup) olive oil
¾ cup sugar	1 ladle (⅓ cup) whiskey
Pinch salt	

Boil anise, orange peel, and milk for 10–15 minutes almost to a boil or scald. Strain the anise and orange from the milk. Add sugar and salt until the sugar is dissolved. Cool. Sift flour and slowly add to the milk mixture. Add the beaten eggs and then the ladles of oil and whiskey. Let stand for 2 hours or overnight. Heat your oiled frying or crepe pan to hot and pour in a thin stream of crepe mixture. If the mixture is too thick add more milk. It must produce thin and light crepes. When done roll and shake granulated sugar over crêpes.

Kings Cake (*Galette des Rois*)

Unlike its Louisiana cousin, the traditional French Kings Cake is served between Christmas Eve and Epiphany (January 6).

⅔ cup sugar	1 Tbsp. rum (optional)
½ cup butter, softened	1 pound puff pastry (2 rounds)

1 cup ground almonds   1 large dry bean or fève figurine

2 eggs + 1 egg for painting

To make the frangipane, blend the butter with the sugar until well combined. Blend in the almonds thoroughly. Beat in the 2 eggs one at a time and then the rum if you are using it.

In a small bowl, beat the remaining egg.

Roll out half of the puff pastry into a round about 12 inches in diameter. Place it on a wax paper–lined baking sheet. Using a pastry brush, paint the outer 1½ inch circumference of the pastry with beaten egg.

Spread the frangipane in a round in the center of the pastry so that it just meets the painted on egg. Press the bean into the frangipane somewhere close to the outer edge.

Place the other puff pastry (rolled out into an equally sized round) on top of the first. Use the times of a fork to press the edges closed. Brush the top of the galette with the beaten egg.

Use a paring knife to etch a pretty pattern into the top of the galette. Traditionally this is in a cross-hatch pattern or concentric half circles, but you can make up your own pattern if you are feeling creative. Don't cut through the pastry, just etch.

Cut a small hole in the center of the pastry to allow steam to escape. Place the galette in the refrigerator to cool for at least 30 minutes before baking. You can make it a day in advance as well—just be sure to keep it refrigerated.

Preheat the oven to 400°F. Place the refrigerated galette in the center of the oven and bake for 30 to 35 minutes or until the top is dark golden brown. Serve warm.

Makes 8 servings.

—*From "Easy French Food," by Kim Steele*

Corn Biscuits (*Biscuits au Mais*)

½ cup butter (room temperature)   2 eggs (room temperature)

⅓ cup sugar   1 tsp. salt

1 cup cornmeal   1½ cups flour (approximate)

In a large bowl stir in broken butter; slowly add sugar and blend until creamy (75 strokes); add cornmeal, eggs, and salt. Beat until smooth; add 1¼ cups of flour. Mixture will be soft and moist; if too sticky add more flour. Roll out to ¼ inch thickness and cut 1½ inch round. Preheat oven to 375°F; bake for 22 minutes, but start checking doneness after 12 minutes. Makes 4 dozen biscuits.

Amer Picon

1 large jigger Amer Picon
½ jigger Grenadine

Place with ice cubes in a 6 oz stem glass or an old-fashioned glass and fill with club soda or carbonated water. Stir well. Add a brandy float and a twist of lemon for the zest. A la santé!

Appendix 3

Foodstuffs at Detroit, 1701–1751

From Timothy J. Kent, *Ft. Pontchartrain at Detroit: A Guide to the Daily Lives of Fur Trade and Military Personnel, Settlers, and Missionaries at French Posts* (Ossineke, MI: Silver Fox Enterprises, 2001), 1:102–13.

Provisions for cooking and eating:

- VEGETABLES: peas, corn, turnips, onions, chives, garlic, raisins, salted green beans
- MEATS: pork, fattened pig, suckling pig, ham, salted beef, veal, deer
- POULTRY: larded chicken, chicken, wild fowl (partridge, turkey, bustard, or swan)
- GRAIN: whole wheat, fine white flour, corn, biscuits, lentils, bran, oats, barley, rice, bread
- DAIRY: butter, eggs, cheese (local, Gruyère, Parmesan)
- FATS: olive oil, tallow, lard, mixed grease, bear oil in buffalo bladder
- BEVERAGES: coffee, brandy; Cyprian, French, Italian, Portuguese, South African, Spanish wines, red and white wine; raspberry and other liqueurs, English beer
- CONDIMENTS AND SPICES: salt, pepper, sugar, vinegar, cloves, nutmeg, brown sugar, cinnamon, salted herbs, capers, anchovies, mushrooms, truffles, lemons, dried oranges, candied lemons, candied fruit, almonds, chocolate, ginseng

French Geographical Legacy in Michigan

FRENCH TERM	ENGLISH TERM	LOCATION
Abbaye	Monastery	Peninsula and point; Baraga County
Allouez	Claude (1622–89); Jesuit missionary	Town; Keweenaw County
Au Gres	Sandstone	Point and town; Arenac County
Au Sable	Sand	Point and town; Isoco and Alger Counties
Au Train	Passage or way	Bay, town, lake, island; Alger County
Belle Isle	Beautiful Island	Wayne County
Bete Grise	Grey Animal	Light, bay, and town; Keweenaw County
Bois Blanc Island	White Wood Island	Mackinac County
Charlevoix	Pierre (1682–1761); Jesuit chronicler-missionary	City and county; Charlevoix County
Brulee Point	Burned Point	Mackinac County
Cadillac	Antoine (1658–1730); founder of Detroit	Wexford County

Detour	Détour: Turning	Mackinac and Delta Counties
Detroit	D'Etroit: Of the Narrows	Wayne County
Epoufette	Stolen Child?	Mackinac County
Goulette Point	Small Narrow Entrance	Macomb County
Grand Marais	Big Swamp	Alger County
Gros Cap	Big Cape	Mackinac County
Grosse Ile	Big Island	Wayne County
Grosse Pointe	Big Point	Mackinac and Wayne Counties
Isle Royale	Royal Island	Houghton County
La Barbe Point	Beard Point	Mackinac County
Lac La Belle	Beautiful Lake	Keweenaw County
L'Anse	Meadow	Town; Baraga County
L'Anse Creuse Bay	Excavated Meadow Bay	Macomb County
Les Cheneaux Islands	Roof eaves	Mackinac County
Marquette	Jacques (1637–75); Jesuit missionary-explorer	City and county; Marquette County
Millecoquins Point	1000 Shell Point	Mackinac County
Mirre Point	Target/Focal Point	Neebish Island, Chippewa County
Pointe aux Barques	Point of the Boats	Huron and Delta Counties
Pointe aux Chenes	Oak Point	Mackinac and St. Clair Counties
Point aux Frenes	Point of Ash Trees	Chippewa County
Pointe Mouillee	Wet Point	Monroe County
Pointe aux Pins	Pine Point	Cheboygan County
Pointe aux Tremble	Shaking/Quaking Point	St. Clair County
Point Detachee	Detached Point	Bois Blanc Island, Mackinac County
Point Hennepin	Louis (1626–ca. 1705); Recollet priest-explorer	Wayne County

Presque Isle	Presqu'ile: Peninsula	Alpena, Marquette, and Presque Isle Counties
Rivière Rouge	Red River	Wayne County
Rivière de Mort	Dead River	Marquette County
St. Ignace	St. Ignatius; founder of the Society of Jesus (Jesuits)	Mackinac County
St. Vital Point	St. Vitus Point	Mackinac County
Sault Ste. Marie	Falls of the St. Mary's River	Chippewa County
Seul Choix	Unaided Selection	Point and lighthouse; Schoolcraft County
Traverse	Short Cut	Point and bay; Grand Traverse, Keweenaw, and Houghton Counties

Notes

1. John P. DuLong, *French Canadians in Michigan* (East Lansing: Michigan State University Press, 2001).

2. Laurie Collier, "French Americans," in *Gale Encyclopedia of Multicultural America*, ed. Judy Galens, Anna Sheets, and Robyn V. Young, 2 vols. (New York: Gale Research, 1995), 1:537.

3. *Sixteenth Census of the United States: 1940. Population*, vol. 2 (Washington, DC: U.S. Government Printing Office, 1943), 777.

4. The term *sieur* or "sir" is a title, and what follows usually refers to a place that the individual was associated with.

5. Harrison J. MacLean, *The Fate of the "Griffon"* (Chicago: Sage Books, 1974).

6. Fort Michilimackinac has been reconstructed, and Fort Mackinac State Historic Park shows what life was like for the early French and English settlers.

7. The Society of Jesus, a Catholic order of priests, was established in 1540 by Ignatius of Loyola. They were dedicated to a ministry to foreign missions, education, and studies in the humanities and sciences.

8. Ernest J. Lajeunesse, "La Richardie, Armand de," *Dictionary of Canadian Biography*, vol. 3 (Toronto: University of Toronto, 1974), 355–56.

9. Ernest J. Lajeunesse, ed., *The Windsor Border Region: Canada's Southernmost Frontier* (Toronto: Champlain Society for the Government of Ontario and the University of Toronto Press, 1960), 21, 42.

10. Russell M. Magnaghi, "The Jesuits of the Lake Superior Country," *Inland Seas* 41, no. 3 (Fall 1985): 190–203.

11. Clarence M. Burton, ed., "The Cadillac Papers," *Michigan Pioneer and Historical Collections* 33 (1903): 36–716; 34 (1904): 11–363.

12. Malcolm MacLeod, "Daneau de Muy, Jacques-Pierre," in *Dictionary of Canadian Biography*, vol. 3 (Toronto: University of Toronto, 1974), 161–63.

13. Robert Navarre, *Journal of Pontiac's Conspiracy, 1763*, ed. M. Agnes Burton, trans. Fred Clyde Ford (Detroit: Michigan Society of the Colonial Wars, 1913).

14. Karen E. Bush, *First Lady of Detroit: The Story of Marie-Thérèse Guyon, Madame Cadillac* (Detroit: Wayne State University Press, 2001).

15. William E. Peters, *Ohio Lands and Their Subdivision* (Athens, OH: W.E. Peters, 1918), 176–83.

16. Friend Palmer, Harry P. Hunt, and Charles Mills June, *Early Days in Detroit* (Detroit: Hunt & June, 1906), 468–71.

17. For general information, see the index of the *Michigan Pioneer and Historical Collections* and Silas Farmer, *History of Detroit and Wayne County and Early Michigan: A Chronological Cyclopedia of the Past and Present* (Detroit: S. Farmer, 1890), 55, 59, 123, 135, 142, 143, 730, 731, 847, 859, 860.

18. Clarence M. Burton, *History of Detroit, 1780–1850; Financial and Commercial* (Detroit: Detroit News, 1917), 19.

19. "Journal of Peter Audrain," *Michigan Pioneer and Historical Collections* 8 (1885): 444–46.

20. Jean Dilhet, État de l'eglise catholique ou diocèse des États-Unis de l'Amérique septentrionale, trans. and annot. Patrick W. Browne (Washington, DC: Salve Regina Press, 1922).

21. Willis F. Dunbar, *Michigan: A History of the Wolverine State* (1965; 3rd rev. ed., Grand Rapids: William B. Eerdmans Publishing, 1995), 110.

22. For an in-depth study of Father Richard, see Frank B. Woodford and Albert Hyma, *Gabriel Richard: Frontier Ambassador* (Detroit: Wayne State University Press, 1958).

23. See Thomas T. McAvoy, *The History of the Catholic Church in the South Bend Area* (South Bend, IN: Aquinas Library and Book Shop, 1953).

24. One of the few studies dealing intimately with the French is Sally Osentoski, "The French in Detroit, 1860" (2011), paper deposited in the Northern Michigan University Archives.

25. Louis-Édouard Rivot, "Voyage au Lac Supérieur, fait en 1854, par Mr. Rivot, en-

génieur des mines," M. Lambert notarie a Paris Place de l'École de medicine, no. 17. Copy deposited in the Library of Congress.

26. Louis-Édouard Rivot, *Voyage au lac Supérieur* (Paris: V. Daimont, 1855); see also Russell M. Magnaghi, ed. and trans., *Selections of Voyage du Lake Superieur by Louis-Edouard Rivot* (Marquette, MI: Belle Fontaine Press, 2003).

27. Louis-Édouard Rivot, *Notice sur le Lac Supérieur, États-Unis d'Amérique* (Paris: V. Dalmont, 1857).

28. *Prospectus of the Lafayette Mining Company, 1864* (New York: Francis Hart, 1864), 2.

29. Don H. Clarke, *Clark Mining Company*, Copper Mines of Keweenaw 3 (privately published, 1974), 3–9; "Clark, Montreal & Bell clippings" file, Calumet & Hecla Abstract Files; "Copper Mines & Mining—Companies—Clark Mining Company," vertical files, Copper Country Historical Collections, Michigan Technological University.

30. C. Harry Benedict, *Red Metal: The Calumet and Hecla Story* (Ann Arbor: University of Michigan Press, 1952), 105–11.

31. *Annual Directory of Detroit for 1876–77*, (Detroit: J.W. Weeks & Company, 1876), 150.

32. *Johnston's Detroit City Directory and Advertising* (Detroit: James Dale Johnston, 1861), 168; *Detroit City Directory* (Detroit: R.L. Polk, 1874), 631; Robert B. Ross and George B. Catlin, *Landmarks of Wayne County and Detroit* (Detroit: The Evening News Association, 1898), 585.

33. Louis Fasquelle, *A New Method of Learning the French Language, Embracing Both the Analytic and Synthetic Modes of Instruction* (New York: M. H. Newman, 1851).

34. "Professor Louis Fasquelle, a Linguist of World Wide Fame," *Michigan Pioneer and Historical Collections* 28 (1897–98): 626–29.

35. *Acts of the Legislature of the State of Michigan, 1861* (Lansing: John A. Kerr, 1861), 585.

36. François Artault's works: *Mines de cuivre du lac Supérieur: Revue retrospective de l'année 1860* (Paris: Impr. de H. Plon, 1861); *Mines du cuivre du comté d'Ontonagon: Lac Supérieur, état du Michigan, États-Unis d'Amérique* (Paris: Henry Plon, 1861); *Exposé d'un projet de création d'un établissement métallurgique au village d'Ontonagon, sur les bords du lac Supérieur, dans l'État du Michigan* (Paris: Impr. de Jules-Juteau, 1862).

37. *Lake Superior Journal*, September 3, 1853; *Portage Lake Mining Gazette*, January

20, 1876, February 17, 1875.

38. *Upper Peninsula Catholic*, March 17, 2006, 7.

39. In the 1920s when Schoolcraft Road was macadamized his youngest son, Eli, asked for the best logs and made a cane and gun rack that remains in the family.

40. Della Mettetal Kunster, *The Genealogical Record of the Mettetal Family, 1728–1965*, (Detroit: n.p., 1976), 4–27.

41. George L. Price, "After the Smoke Cleared!" *Gateway* 23, no. 1 (August 1914): 31–32; *Marquette Mining Journal*, July 20, 1929, 4; *Marquette Mining Journal*, July 24, 1929, 4; *Calumet News*, July 23, 3.

42. Paul Delarue, ed., and Austin E. Fife, trans., *The Borzoi Book of French Tales* (New York: Alfred A. Knopf, 1956), xiv.

43. Richard M. Dorson, *Bloodstoppers and Bearwalkers: Folk Traditions of Michigan's Upper Peninsula*, 3rd ed., ed. James P. Leary (Madison: University of Wisconsin Press, 2008), 69–70, 282–83.

44. *Detroit Post*, August 3, 1869.

45. *Detroit Free Press*, February 14, 1855.

46. *Detroit Free Press*, September 17, 1874.

47. Detroit had seventeen newspapers, Bay City seven, Lake Linden three, Marquette two, Muskegon two, Ludington one, and Saginaw one. See Georges J. Joyaux, "French Press in Michigan," *Michigan History* 37, no. 2 (June 1953): 158.

48. A complete run of the rare *Le Citoyen* can be found in the Burton Historical Collection, Detroit Public Library.

49. Louis J. Rosenberg, "Story of the Consular Corps of Detroit," *Michigan History* 23, no. 2 (Spring–Summer 1939): 365–74.

50. James T. Schleifer, *The Making of Tocqueville's Democracy in America* (Chapel Hill: The University of North Carolina Press, 1980), 62, 64, 65, 67, 71, 309; George W. Pierson, *Tocqueville and Beaumont in America* (New York: Oxford University Press, 1938; repr., Baltimore, MD: Johns Hopkins University Press, 1996), 45, 48, 53, 62, 64, 76, 237; and Alexis de Tocqueville, "A Fortnight in the Wilderness," in Justin L. Kestenbaum, ed., *The Making of Michigan: 1820–1860: A Pioneer Anthology*, 17–56 (Detroit: Wayne State University Press, 1990).

51. Howard H. Peckham, "The Reverend Mr. Williams Dauphin of France," *Quarterly Review* 69, no. 11 (December 1942): 60–68.

52. Philippe Édouard Poulletier de Verneuil, "Note sur le parallélisme des roches dépôts paléozoiques . . . ," *Societé Geologique de France Bulletin* 4 (1847): 646–710.

53. Camille Ferri Pisani, *Prince Napoleon in America, 1861: Letters from His Aide-du-Camp*, trans. Georges J. Joyaux (Bloomington: Indiana University Press, 1959).

54. For a study of Ford's role in the development of Renault, see Anthony Rhodes, *Louis Renault, a Biography* (New York: Harcourt, Brace & World, 1969), 66–74.

55. John Reynolds, *André Citroën, Engineer, Explorer, Entrepreneur* (Sparkford: Haynes Publishing, 2006).

56. Pierre Barras, *The Louis Chevrolet Adventure* (Detroit: Chevrolet, 2004); "Louis Chevrolet," *Your Dictionary*, http://biography.your dictionary-chevrolet; Ralph Kramer, "Louis Chevrolet: His Gift Was Cars, Not Corporations," *Automotive News*, October 21, 2011, http://autonews.com-Louis Chevrolet; Marti Benedetti, "Gifted Race Car Driver, Inventor, Died Penniless and Forgotten," *Automotive News*, September 14, 2011, http://autonews.com-Louis Chevrolet.

57. "French Originate Nomenclature of Motor Car, Yanks Built Them," *Detroit News*, May 29, 1921, 8.

58. At this time the office was located at 610–611 Union Trust Building, Detroit.

59. Some of the French immigrants and their occupations: Gabriel Cau was waiter at the Hotel Cadillac; Henri Moreau was employed at the Detroit Screw Works; Louis Laz was employed at the Morgan & Wright factory.

60. *Detroit News*, August 4, 1914, 5; August 8, 1914, 14.

61. *Detroit News*, August 8, 1914, 5.

62. *Detroit News*, August 6, 1914, 10.

63. Books highlighted on France included J. U. Higinbotham, *Three Weeks in France* (Chicago: Reilly & Britton, 1913); Charles Bastide, *The Anglo-French Entente in the Seventeenth Century* (London: John Lane, 1914); Cecil Headlam, *France* (London: A. & C. Black, 1913); A. Vizetelly, *Republican France, 1870–1912: Her Presidents, Statesmen, Policy, Vicissitudes and Social Life* (Boston: Small, Maynard, 1913); E. B. Washburne, *Recollections of a Minister to France, 1869–1877* (New York: C. Scribner's Sons, 1887); Mary King Waddington, *My First Years as a Frenchwoman, 1876–1879* (New York: C. Scribner's Sons, 1914); and Raymond Poincaré, *How France Is Governed* (Port Washington, NY: Kennikat Press, 1970). This list of books was taken from *Detroit News*, August 4, 1914, 7.

64. Grace Mendiara Magnaghi (1911–2011), a California and then Marquette resident, continued to remember and privately celebrate the day with a round of "La Marseillaise" and a special restaurant dinner into her late nineties.

65. *Detroit Free Press Tribune*, July 13 and 15, 1902.

66. *Detroit News*, July 15, 1918, Pt. 2, 1.

67. *Detroit News*, July 14, 1921, Pt. 2, 1; 4.

68. *Detroit News*, July 15, 1940, 6.

69. *Detroit Free Press*, July 16, 2000.

70. *Detroit News*, November 11, 1921, 2.

71. Detroit News, November 7, 1921, 2.

72. "The 'French Women Benevolent Club' anciennement 'French War Brides Club,' Detroit, 1946," International Institute Box 11, Folder 5, Archives of Labor and Urban Affairs, Wayne State University, Detroit.

73. "The Huguenot Society of Michigan," in Frances Marie Bryant Papers, Bentley Library, University of Michigan, Ann Arbor.

74. Wayne County communities: Detroit (1,759), Dearborn (73), Highland Park (51), Grosse Pointe Park (30), Ecorse (10), Hamtramck (10), River Rouge (8), Lincoln Park (6), and Wyandotte (6).

75. This section is based on the interview with Raymonde D found in Hilary Kaiser's *French War Brides in America: An Oral History* (Westport, CT: Praeger, 2008), personal interviews, and research from the Reuther Library, Wayne State University.

76. Jean-Philippe Mousnier, *Paul Paray* (Paris: Editions L'Harmattan, 1998); Jean Cabon, "Paul Paray, 1886–1979: French Composer and Conductor," Paul Paray, http://paulparay.com; Arthur Boomfield, *More than the Notes: The Conducting of Toscanini, Furtwaenger, Skokowski and Friends*, More than the Notes, chapter 60, http://www.morethanthenotes.com/.

77. *Marquette Mining Journal*, March 9, 2003.

For Further Reference

Acts of the Legislature of the State of Michigan, 1861. Lansing: John A. Kerr, 1861.

Allen, James P., and Eugene J. Turner. *We the People: An Atlas of America's Ethnic Diversity.* New York: Macmillan, 1988.

Alleman, F. R. "The Alsatians." *Encounter* 23, no. 5 (November 1964): 45–54.

Anderson, Malcolm. "Regional Identity and Political Change: The Case of Alsace from the Third to the Fifth Republic." *Political Studies* 20, no. 1 (March 1972): 17–30.

Annual Directory of Detroit for 1876–77. Detroit: J.W. Weeks & Company, 1876.

Archibald, Robert, ed. *Northern Border: History and Lore of Michigan's Upper Peninsula and Beyond.* Marquette: Northern Michigan University Press, 2014.

Artault, François. *Mines de cuivre du lac Supérieur: Revue retrospective de l'année 1860.* Paris: Impr. de H. Plon, 1861.

———. *Mines du cuivre du comté d'Ontonagon: Lac Supérieur, état du Michigan, États-Unis d'Amérique.* Paris: Henry Plon, 1861.

———. *Exposé d'un projet de création d'un établissement métallurgique au village d'Ontonagon, sur les bords du lac Supérieur, dans l'État du Michigan.* Paris: Impr. de Jules-Juteau, 1862.

Bak, Richard. "The French Connection." *Hour Detroit*, July 2001.

Bald, F. Clever. *Gabriel Richard, the First Vice-President of the University of Michigan.* Bulletin of the Michigan Historical Collections 2. Ann Arbor: University of Michigan, 1948.

Baroux, Louis. *Correspondence of Rev. Louis Baroux, Missionary Apostolic of Michigan, to Rev. M.J. DeNeve, Superior of the American College at Louvain.* Translated from French by Edward Kelly. Ann Arbor: Ann Arbor Press, 1913.

———. *Notice sur la mission des Pottowatomies dans l'état du Michigan.* Caen: A. Hardel, 1858.

Barras, Pierre. *The Louis Chevrolet Adventure.* Detroit: Chevrolet, 2004.

Bates, George C. "By-Gones of Detroit." *Michigan Pioneer and Historical Collections* 22 (1894): 305–404.

Benedetti, Marti. "Gifted Race Car Driver, Inventor, Died Penniless and Forgotten." *Automotive News.* September 14, 2011. Http://autonews.com-Louis Chevrolet.

Benedict, C. Harry. *Red Metal: The Calumet and Hecla Story.* Ann Arbor: University of Michigan Press, 1952.

Bertier de Sauvigny, Guillaume de, and David H. Pinkney. *History of France.* Translated by James Friguglietti. Wheeling, IL: Forum Press, 1983.

Braun, Lilian Jackson. "That Bit of Paris in Our Town." *Detroit Free Press*, February 7, 1965.

Bredvold, L. I. "A Note on La Hontan and the *Encyclopédie.*" *Modern Language Notes* 47 (1932): 508–9.

Brown, Henry D., et al. *Cadillac and the Founding of Detroit: Commemorating the Two Hundred and Seventy-fifth Anniversary of the Founding of the City of Detroit by Antoine Laumet de Lamothe Cadillac on July 24, 1701.* Detroit: Wayne State University Press, 1976.

Bunle, Henri. "L'Immigration française aux États-Unis." *Bulletin de la statistique générale de la France* 14 (January 1925): 199–222.

Burton, Clarence M., ed. "The Cadillac Papers." *Michigan Pioneer and Historical Collections* 33 (1903), and 34 (1904).

———. *History of Detroit, 1780–1850; Financial and Commercial.* Detroit: Detroit News, 1917.

Bush, Karen E. *First Lady of Detroit: The Story of Marie-Thérèse Guyon, Madame Cadillac.* Detroit: Wayne State University Press, 2001.

Campbell, James V. "Early French Settlements in Michigan." *Michigan Pioneer and Historical Collections* 2 (1879): 95–104.

Carroll, Raymonde. *Cultural Misunderstandings: The French-American Experience.* Translated by Carol Volk. Chicago: University of Chicago Press, 1988.

Chambers, Frances. *France.* World Bibliographical Series 13. Santa Barbara: Clio Press, 1990.

Chaput, Donald. "French Interest in Lake Superior Copper." *Inland Seas* 26, no. 1 (spring 1970): 20–35.

Charlevoix, S.J., Pierre de. *Journal of a Voyage to North-America.* 2 vols. Anonymously translated into English. London: Printed for R. and J. Dodsley, 1761; repr., New York: Readex Microprint, 1966.

Chevalier, L. "L'Émigration française au XIXe siècle." *Études d'histoire moderne et contemporaire* 1 (1947): 127–71.

Clarke, Don H. *Clark Mining Company.* Copper Mines of Keweenaw 3. Privately published, 1974.

Collier, Laurie. "French Americans." In *Gale Encyclopedia of Multicultural America*, ed. Judy Galens, Anna Sheets, and Robyn V. Young, 1:533–45. New York: Gale Research, 1995.

Combes, Charles. "Discours prononcé aux funerailles de M. Rivot, le 25 fevrier 1869." *Annales des Mines* 6e série, 25 (1869): 205–7.

Cooper, Leigh G. "Influence of the French Inhabitants of Detroit upon Its Early Political Life." *Michigan History* 4, no. 1 (January 1920): 299–304.

Daniels, Roger. *Coming to America: A History of Immigration and Ethnicity in American Life.* 2nd ed. New York: Harper/Perennial, 2002.

Delanglez, S.J., Jean. "Genesis and Building of Detroit." *Mid-America* 30 (1948): 75–96.

Delarue, Paul, ed., and Austin E. Fife, trans. *The Borzoi Book of French Tales.* New York: Alfred A. Knopf, 1956.

Detroit City Directory. Detroit: R.L. Polk, 1874.

DuLong, John P. *French Canadians in Michigan.* East Lansing: Michigan State University Press, 2001.

Dilhet, Jean. État de l'eglise catholique ou *diocèse des États-Unis de l'Amérique septentrionale.* Translated and annotated by Patrick W. Browne. Washington, DC: Salve Regina Press, 1922.

Dodenhoff, Jean. "Grosse Pointe' First Settlers: From Whence Did They Come?" *Tonnancour* 2 (1995): 20–28.

Dorson, Richard M. *Bloodstoppers and Bearwalkers: Folk Traditions of Michigan's Upper Peninsula.* Cambridge, MA: Harvard University Press, 1952; 3rd ed. James P. Leary, editor, Madison: University of Wisconsin Press, 2008.

Donnelly, Joseph P. *Jacques Marquette, S.J., 1637–1675.* Chicago: Loyola University Press, 1968.

Dunbar, Willis F. *Michigan: A History of the Wolverine State.* 1965; 3rd rev. ed., Grand Rapids: William B. Eerdsmans Publishing, 1995.

Elliott, Richard R. "The Jesuits of L'Ancien Regime Who Labored on Michigan Soil—
Their Detractors." *American Catholic Quarterly Review* 28 (1903): 90–114.

Farmer, Silas. *History of Detroit and Wayne County and Early Michigan: A Chronological Cyclopedia of the Past and Present.* Detroit: S. Farmer, 1890.

———. "The Old French Pear Trees." *Tonnancour* 1 (1994): 30–32.

Fasquelle, Louis. *A New Method of Learning the French Language, Embracing Both
the Analytic and Synthetic Modes of Instruction.* New York: M. H. Newman, 1851.

Ferri Pisani, Camille. *Prince Napoleon in America, 1861: Letters from His Aide-de-
Camp.* Translated by Georges J. Joyaux. Bloomington: Indiana University Press,
1959.

Fournier, Martin. *Jardins et potagers en Nouvelle-France: Joie de vivre et patrimoine
culinaire.* Sillery: Éditions du Septentrion, 2004.

Gauthier, Donat, and George Graff. "French." In *Ethnic Groups in Michigan,* ed.
James M. Anderson and Iva A. Smith, Peoples of Michigan 2:119–24. Detroit:
Ethnos Press, Michigan Ethnic Heritage Studies Center and the University of
Michigan Ethnic Studies Program, 1983.

Geismar, Leo M. *The Upper Peninsula of Michigan.* Marquette, MI: The Upper Peninsula Development Bureau, 1920.

Girardin, J. A. "Life and Times of Rev. Gabriel Richard." *Michigan Pioneer and Historical Collections* 1 (1876): 481–95.

Greenly, A. H. "Lahontan: An Essay and Bibliography." *Papers of the Bibliographical
Society of America* 48 (1954): 334–89.

———. *A Bibliography of Father Richard's Press in Detroit.* Ann Arbor: University of
Michigan Press, 1955.

Hamil, Fred Coyne. "The French Heritage of the Detroit Region." *Michigan History* 47,
no. 1 (March 1963): 27–33.

———. "The Detroit River French." *Western Ontario Historical Notes* 3, no. 2 (June
1945): 27–33.

Hamlin, Marie Caroline W. "Old French Traditions." *Michigan Pioneer and Historical
Collections* 4 (1883): 70–78.

———. *Legends of Le Détroit.* Detroit: Thorndike Nourse, 1884.

Hayne, David M. "Louis-Armand de Lom d'Arce de Lahontan." In *Dictionary of Canadian Biography,* 2:439–44. Toronto: University of Toronto Press, 1969.

———. "Pierre-François Xavier Charlevoix." In *Dictionary of Canadian Biography,*
3:103–10. Toronto: University of Toronto Press, 1969.

Hickey, Edward J. *Ste. Anne's Parish: One Hundred Years of Detroit History.* Detroit:

Wayne State University Press, 1951.

Higonnet, Patrick Louis René. "French." In *Harvard Encyclopedia of American Ethnic Groups*, ed. Stephan Thernstrom, 379–88. Cambridge, MA: Harvard University Press, 1980.

Holli, Melvin G., ed. *Detroit*. New York: New Viewpoints, 1976.

Hubbard, Bela. *Memorials of a Half-Century in Michigan and the Lake Region*. New York: G. P. Putnam's Sons, 1888.

Innis, Harold A. *The Fur Trade in Canada: An Introduction to Canadian Economic History*. New Haven: Yale University Press, 1930.

Johnston's Detroit City Directory and Advertising. Detroit: James Dale Johnston, 1861.

Joyeaux, Georges J. "French Press in Michigan: A Bibliography." *Michigan History* 36, no. 3 (September 1952): 260–78.

Kaiser, Hilary. *French War Brides in America: An Oral History*. Westport, CT: Praeger, 2008.

Keller, Velera. "An Early Visitor to Michigan, Charlevoix," *Michigan History* 12, no. 2 (April 1928): 252–66.

Kellogg, Louise P. *The French Régime in Wisconsin and the Northwest*. Madison: State Historical Society of Wisconsin, 1925.

Kent, Timothy J. *Rendezvous at the Straits: Fur Trade and Military Activities at Fort de Buade and Fort Michilimackinac, 1669–1781*. 2 vols. Ossineke, MI: Silver Fox Enterprises, 2004.

———. *Ft. Pontchartrain at Detroit: A Guide to the Daily Lives of Fur Trade and Military Personnel, Settlers, and Missionaries at French Posts*. 2 vols. Ossineke, MI: Silver Fox Enterprises, 2001.

Kimes, Beverly Rae, and Robert C. Ackerson. *Chevrolet: A History from 1911*. [Kutztown, PA]: Automobile Quarterly Publications, 1984.

Kramer, Ralph. "Louis Chevrolet: His Gift Was Cars, Not Corporations." *Automotive News*. October 21, 2011. Http://autonews.com-Louis Chevrolet.

Kunster, Della Mettetal. *The Genealogical Record of the Mettetal Family, 1728–1965*. Detroit: n.p., 1967, 4–27.

Lajeunesse, Ernest J., ed. *The Windsor Border Region: Canada's Southernmost Frontier*. Toronto: Champlain Society for the Government of Ontario and the University of Toronto Press, 1960.

———. "La Richardie, Armand de." In *Dictionary of Canadian Biography*, 3:355–56. Toronto: University of Toronto Press, 1974.

Langworth, Richard M., and Jan P. Norbye. *Chevrolet, 1911–1985*. Skokie, IL: Publications International; New York: Beekman House, 1984.

Leacock, Stephen. "Baron de Lahontan, Explorer." *Canadian Geographical Journal* 4 (1932): 281–94.

Lewis, Ferris E. *Detroit: A Wilderness Outpost of Old France.* Detroit: Wayne University Press, 1951.

"Louis Chevrolet." *Your Dictionary.* Http://biography.your dictionary-chevrolet.

Lyman, David. "Bonjour Detroit." *Detroit Free Press,* July 13, 1999.

MacLean, Harrison J. *The Fate of the "Griffon."* Chicago: Sage Books, 1974.

MacLeod, Malcolm. "Daneau de Muy, Jacques-Pierre." In *Dictionary of Canadian Biography,* 3:161–63. Toronto: University of Toronto Press, 1974.

McAvoy, Thomas T. *The History of the Catholic Church in the South Bend Area.* South Bend, IN: Aquinas Library and Book Shop, 1953.

Magnaghi, Russell M. "The Jesuits in the Lake Superior Country." *Inland Seas* 41, no. 3 (fall 1985): 190–203.

———. "Point aux Pins: Lake Superior's First Industrial Center." *Preview* 6, no. 1 (January 1986): 6–7.

———. "Jacques Marquette, S.J. in the Upper Peninsula, 1668–1673." *Peninsula Heritage* 1, no. 1 (winter 1987): 2–3.

———. "Fort Buade" (p. 82), "Fort Miami" (p. 437), "Fort Michilimackinac" (pp. 438–39), "Fort Pontchartrain de Detroit" (pp. 570–71), and "Fort St. Joseph-St. Clair River" (p. 654). In *Colonial Wars of North America, 1512–1763: An Encyclopedia,* ed. Alan Gallay, Military History of the United States 5. New York: Garland Press, 1996.

———, ed. and trans. *Selections of Voyage du Lake Superieur by Louis-Edouard Rivot.* Marquette, MI: Belle Fontaine Press, 2003.

Magnaghi, Russell, et al., compilers. *Immigrants and Their Occupations in Michigan's Upper Peninsula: The Federal Census, 1910.* Center for Upper Peninsula Studies, Occasional Publication 2. Marquette: Northern Michigan University, 2009.

Massignon, Geneviève, ed. *Folktales of France.* Translated by Jacqueline Hyland. Chicago: University of Chicago Press, 1968.

May, George S., ed. *The Automobile Industry, 1920–1980.* Vol. 8 of *Encyclopedia of American Business History and Biography.* New York: Facts on File, 1989.

———. *The Mess at Mackinac or, No More Sagamity for Me, Thank You!* Mackinac Island, MI: Mackinac Island State Park Commission, 1964.

Mitchell, Patricia B. *French Cooking in Early America.* Chatham, VA: Privately Published, 1991.

Monroe, J. J. "Regional Variation in French Emigration Rates." *International Migra-tion* 4, nos. 3/4 (1966): 186–97.

Mousnier, Jean-Philippe. *Paul Paray*. Paris: Editions L'Harmattan, 1998.

Navarre, Robert. *Journal of Pontiac's Conspiracy, 1763*. Edited by M. Agnes Burton. Translated by Fred Clyde Ford. Detroit: Michigan Society of The Colonial Wars, 1913.

Nute, Grace Lee. *The Voyageur*. New York: D. Appleton, 1931.

Osentoski, Sally. "The French in Detroit, 1860" (2011). Paper deposited in the Northern Michigan University Archives.

Palmer, Friend, Harry P. Hunt, and Charles Mills June. *Early Days in Detroit*. Detroit: Hunt & June, 1906.

Paré, George W. *The Catholic Church in Detroit, 1701–1888*. Detroit: Gabriel Richard Press, 1951.

Peckham, Howard H. "The Reverend Mr. Williams Dauphin of France." *Quarterly Review* 69, no. 11 (December 1942): 60–68.

Peters, William E. *Ohio Lands and Their Subdivision*. Athens, OH: W. E. Peters, 1918.

Petersen, Eugene T. *France at Mackinac: A Pictorial Record of French Life and Culture, 1715–1760*. Mackinac Island, MI: Mackinac Island State Park Commission, 1968.

Pierson, George W. *Tocqueville and Beaumont in America*. New York: Oxford University Press, 1938; repr., Baltimore, MD: Johns Hopkins University Press, 1996.

Pierson, George W., and James T. Scheifer. *The Making of Tocqueville's Democracy in America*. Chapel Hill: The University of North Carolina Press, 1980.

Price, George L. "After the Smoke Cleared!" *Gateway* 23, no. 1 (August 1914): 31–32.

"Professor Louis Fasquelle, a Linguist of World Wide Fame." *Michigan Pioneer and Historical Collections* 28 (1897–98): 626–29.

Prospectus of the Lafayette Mining Company, 1864. New York: Francis Hart, 1864.

Radike, Floyd D. *Detroit: A French Village on the Frontier*. Detroit: Wayne University Press, 1951.

Reynolds, John. *André Citroën, Engineer, Explorer, Entrepreneur*. Sparkford: Haynes Publishing, 2006.

Rezek, Antoine Ivan. *History of the Diocese of Sault Ste. Marie and Marquette*. 2 vols. Houghton, MI: Privately printed, 1906–7.

Rhodes, Anthony. *Louis Renault, a Biography*. New York: Harcourt, Brace & World, 1969.

Riddell, William R. "When Detroit Was French." *Michigan History* 28, no. 1 (Winter1939), 37–52.

————. "A Late Official Report on the French Posts in the Northern Part of North America." *Michigan History* 16, no. 1 (Winter 1932): 68–81.

Rivot, Louis-Édouard. *Voyage au lac Supérieur.* Paris: V. Dalmont, 1855.

————. *Notice sur le Lac Supérieur, États-Unis d'Amérique.* Paris: V. Dalmont, 1857.

Robb, Graham. *The Discovery of France: A Historical Geography from the Revolution to the First World War.* New York: W. W. Norton, 2007.

Rosenberg, Louis J. "Story of the Consular Corps of Detroit." *Michigan History* 23, no. 2 (Spring–Summer, 1939): 365–74.

Ross, Robert B., and George B. Catlin. *Landmarks of Wayne County and Detroit.* Detroit: The Evening News Association, 1898.

Ruskowski, Leo F. *French Émigré Priests in the United States (1791–1812).* Washington, DC: Catholic University of America Press, 1940.

Sands, Walter M. "Leo Geismar." *Find A Grave.* July 11, 2013.

Schauinger, J. Herman. *Stephen T. Badin, Priest in the Wilderness.* Milwaukee: Bruce Publishing, 1956.

Schleifer, James T. *The Making of Tocqueville's Democracy in America.* Chapel Hill: The University of North Carolina Press, 1980.

Schermerhorn, Jane. "Her Boss Arrived with Two Concubines." *Detroit News*, March 5, 1967.

Sheryl, James. "French Connection: A Noted But Faded Legacy of City." *Detroit Free Press*, August 24, 2000.

Sixteenth Census of the United States: 1940. Population. Vol. 2. Washington, DC: U.S. Government Printing Office, 1943.

Stephenson, Larry W. "Tonnacour's Roots Found in France." *The Moorings* 17, no. 1 (spring 2000): 6–9.

Stephenson, Larry W., and René Beaudoin. "In Search of Tonnacour." *The Moorings* 16, no. 1 (spring 1999): 9–20.

"Sur M. Gabriel Richard, Vicaire-General." *Le Citoyen* 1, no. 12 (August 3, 1850): [89]–90; 1, no. 13 (August 10, 1850): 97–98; 1, no. 14 (August 17, 1850): 105–6; 1, no. 15 (August 24, 1850): 113–14.

Thwaites, Reuben G. *Father Marquette.* New York: D. Appleton, 1902.

————. *The Jesuit Relations and Allied Documents.* 73 vols. New York: Pageant Books, 1959.

Tocqueville, Alexis de. "A Fortnight in the Wilderness." In *The Making of Michigan, 1820–1860: A Pioneer Anthology*, edited by Justin L. Kestenbaum, 17–56. Detroit: Wayne State University Press, 1990.

———. *A Fortnight in the Wilderness*. Delray Beach, FL: Levenger Press, 1959.

Upper Peninsula Catholic (diocesan weekly).

Vander Hill, C. Warren. *Settling the Great Lakes Frontier: Immigration to Michigan, 1837–1924*. Lansing: Michigan Historical Commission, 1970.

Walling, Regis. "One Woman with Courage: Mother Mary Xavier Le Biham." *Peninsula Heritage* 1, no. 1 (winter 1987): 4–5.

Weadock, Thomas A. E. "A Catholic Priest in Congress—Sketch of Rev. Gabriel Richard." *Michigan Pioneer and Historical Collections* 21 (1894): 432–47.

Woodford, Arthur M., ed. *Tonnancour: Life in Grosse Pointe and along the Shores of Lake St. Clair*. Detroit: Omnigraphics, 1994.

Woodford, Frank B., and Albert Hyma. *Gabriel Richard: Frontier Ambassador*. Detroit: Wayne State University Press, 1958.

Zeman, David. "Fried about the French." *Detroit Free Press*, February 19, 2003.

Zunz, Olivier, ed. *Alexis de Tocqueville and Gustave de Beaumont: Their Friendship and Their Travels*. Translated by Arthur Goldammer. Charlotte: University of Virginia Press, 2010.

Index